Blue Water Dreaming

DEDICATION

This book is dedicated to all those who dream, but especially to those who make their dreams come true like my great-grandparents Bridget and Patrick. Born in Ireland just prior to the potato famine, they married in Lincoln, England where they lived until eventually sailing from Plymouth with their family onboard the *SS Eastminster* in 1886, bound for Australia. Their dream was for a new and better life in Maryborough, Queensland, which they reached after a voyage of 93 days. There are many hundreds of their descendants spread throughout Australia who can thank these two people for the life they now have in this great country of their dreams.

Dare to dream
Dare to do
Dare to make your dreams come true

You can take the sailor from the sea,
But you can never take the sea from the sailor.

Blue Water Dreaming

John Rodgers

PEACOCK
Publications

Further copies of this book are available from:

John Rodgers
6 Crawford Crescent
Mannum
South Australia 5238

Mobile: 0407 392 075
Email: sales@bluewaterdreaming.com.au
Web: www.bluewaterdreaming.com.au

Published in Australia by Peacock Publications
38 Sydenham Road, Norwood, South Australia 5067
Copyright © 2003 John Rodgers
First published August, 2003
National Library of Australia Card Number & ISBN 1 876087 73 0
Designed and produced by Peacock Publications, Adelaide
Printed in Australia by Peacock Publications

Contents

The Crew:
John Rodgers (sitting)
Douglas Dufty (standing)

The Skipper:
Bill Corbett

Chapter One

The Dream

It is only fitting that I start this record of events in a place called Pokororo in the Graham Valley fifteen miles from Motueka at the top of the South Island, New Zealand. It was here that so many things happened to change my life. It was one winter's day in 1958 while I was working in the hop fields clearing and mounding the roots that I made a decision and the dream was started.

Pokoroko, South Island, New Zealand.

It was always the coldest part of the day waiting for the sun to come up from behind the hill and thaw out the frozen ground in the garden. The day began just like any other, start work at eight o clock at one end of the hop field and look down the row three quarters of a mile long, knowing that it would take me until lunch time to get to the end of the first row.

It was a monotonous job clearing the hard, frozen earth from the mounds, and as with any boring job I did it automatically. My mind was on another plane thinking of many things, of life itself, my life and the things that had governed and changed it. All living things began life as a single cell organism millions of years ago and I was here because my ancestors had survived not only the Ice Age but every change the earth had made, every challenge. I thought about the Stone Age man who had plunged his stone-tipped spear into the backbone of a dinosaur that had been found encased in stone. Did he survive? Was he trying to save someone? I can never know, but he did what he had to do.

From the time we are born many things change our lives, the climate and conditions in which we live, the work we do, the books we read and what we are told and taught, not all of it correct and I often wonder why. Why? I knew that I was not the first and would not be the last to ask this question. Perhaps it would be better if I did not think too much, man is what he is and only he can change himself, at least he can grow from less to more. As I worked, my thoughts were interrupted by the sound of a big semi-trailer speeding along the road and when I looked up I saw that there were a couple of hitch-hikers on top of the load.

I wondered where they were going and thought of the many times that I had travelled just as they were. I was tired of living out of a kit-bag and sleeping under trees and bridges. Many times I had thought of owning a small boat, and so began my dream of how it would be to live on one and go wherever you wanted to on the sea and still have something you could call home. As I watched the semi-trailer disappear down the road, I made up my mind there and then that I would buy a boat. I knew that there would be many obstacles, and the first big one would be saving the money, as I was working a day here and there to keep me going until the tobacco season started again in two months time.

When the season opened, I made the decision to grow one acre for myself and look after it when I was not working, weekends and in any other spare time that I might have. I hoped that enough money could be made out of it to put a deposit on my boat. As it turned out I sold my crop for sixty pounds on paper, and collected fifteen pounds in cash, out of which I had to pay the local garage a few quid because of the old bomb that I owned. That year was a dead loss and my boat was put on hold. The only good thing was that I met a chap called DOUGLAS DUFTY, otherwise known as Darkey or Duff. As soon as we shook hands it was like meeting an old friend though I knew that we had never met, well not in this life. We shared many jars of beer while he listened to my boat dreaming and the beaut thing was that he was a great cook and he could drink as much beer as I could.

The only way I knew I could save the money was to go back out in the bush again. I had saved hundreds of pounds in my life, but as I had no point or aim in keeping it, I just wasted the lot. I really didn't want to go bush again, I had spent too long there already, fencing, station work, mining and droving in Australia. Finally the boat won and I took a job at a mine not far from the little valley where I lived, and I stayed there nineteen long months.

I did not come out of the bush very often and spent most of my time back in the mountains, prospecting and bush walking. I usually stayed in Chaffey's hut close to the mine at Upper Takaka. This old prospector had died alone one cold winter's night, on the track after he had fallen and broken his leg. Sometimes I followed the Balloon Creek track and slept in the old miner's hut at the Flora saddle. One of my favourite places was the Tablelands where, at 4000 feet, there was often snow on the tussock grass. I slept in the Salisbury hut when it was cold and in the rock shelter when it was not, and explored the pot-holes and caves. Once, following a small creek, I found a large rock shelter with wood still stacked up and a four-foot cast-iron camp oven that would have been carried in relays on a pole by the old miners. I did one trip to the Leslie Valley to see the Roaring Lion river and stayed in the hut there, that is until the sand-flies drove me back to the high country.

My job as quarry foreman up at the mine was hard and dangerous. One third of the quarry had collapsed in a landslide, thousands of tons of rock and earth had to be moved from the floor, and half way up the walls boulders had to be drilled and blasted. Sometimes they rolled down on us without warning bringing tons of loose earth and rocks that made us run for our lives. It took six months to clear this one slip and my guardian angel was putting in for overtime. I found it quite a change to be working in snow and ice when I was used to the dry, dusty, desert country in Australia. It still got hot in the quarry during the summer. At times our crowbars were too hot to touch and in the winter our hands stuck to them with ice. Swinging a fifteen-pound spalling hammer was never my preferred method of exercise.

It was on one of the trips I made out to the valley to see Duff that I met another bloke who was interested in small boats and sailing. He was a quietly spoken chap from Yarmouth, Isle of Wight, by the name of BILL CORBETT, and so much did he love talking about boats that I nicknamed him 'Boatie'. Bill was born in Penarth, Wales, and lived most of his life on Coast-guard Stations around different parts of the English coast. At the mine I liked working with the stone and would have enjoyed the work except for the boss who was the only man I have met in my life about whom I could not find one redeeming feature; then perhaps I did not look deep enough. I stuck it out because I wanted my boat, but when I sat on the bunk in my hut with five hundred pounds in my hand, I wondered if it was really worth it. When I left the mine it was like getting out of prison.

I went back to the valley again and worked for two weeks hoeing tobacco, then I started looking for my boat. The "Wanted To Buy" ad. I had put in the paper brought no response, so I packed my old kit-bag and started hitch-hiking around the top of the South Island, then over Cook Strait to the North Island, up the West Coast to Whangerai and then back down the East coast. There were no boats to be had for the money that I offered, so I would put on my pack, spit and push on. The weather was not the best, it rained nearly all the time I was on the road.

One day as I walked up a steep hill with my canvas fly over my shoulders, feeling the water run down my neck and my wet pants sticking to my legs, I was a little discouraged until I saw a big sign outside a little country church "Disappointments should be Cremated not Embalmed" and that was the only thing that I got for my searching. As I got closer to Nelson I made up my mind that if I could not find a boat there, I would go over to Takaka and buy a fishing-boat that was for sale.

In Nelson I looked at a boat that I thought may suit me, the price was right but there was one catch, it would not be available for another week. I had the cash on me but that did not help. When I started out I had gone to the bank and changed my money into five one-hundred-pound notes but the teller did not want to give them to me. He warned me they could be stolen, so I put my fists up in front of him and assured him they would not. I made my way back into the valley and down to Pokororo where I had the good fortune of running into Bill. He offered to come to Nelson with me and have a look at the boat. As he was a shipwright and boat builder by trade, I was pleased to accept his offer

I had been in the Royal Australian Navy for several years and served aboard HMAS 'Australia'. This old battle-cruiser was hit by a number of Kamikaze planes and survived them all. I was aboard HMAS 'Culgoa' when she fired her last shots of the Korean War with a 37-round bombardment of 4-inch shells at Communist troops invading the island of Youngmae Do. Whilst on this River Class frigate I experienced two typhoons that taught me respect for the sea and all natural forces that cool and shape our planet. What I knew about sailing would fit on the head of a pin. I had only been sailing once, in a Navy Whaler in Port Philip Bay, and was impressed when the helmsman pulled a bit of string, the sail stopped flapping and the boat moved through the water. In Nelson, Bill looked at the boat and remarked what a beautiful-shaped hull. I thought my search was over but, as he pointed out the things that were wrong with her, I knew that she was not the boat to sail solo across the Tasman to Australia. It had always been my dream to sail alone, but I now knew that I would be lucky to find a boat in New Zealand with the money I had. I was impatient and did not want to wait any longer.

It was Christmas and the valley was the only place I wanted to be, among the people that I knew. With the festive season over, I decided to work in the tobacco again until I made up my mind where to look next. I had worked in the weed on and off for a few years. No matter where I went I always returned to Pokororo. I found the valley a beautiful place, one of the prettiest that I have ever seen, and will always remember the morning when I woke up and walked outside the batch. The valley looked as if at one time it could have been a gigantic lake before the slow-moving mass of a glacier cut its path through there, levelling and grinding, leaving moraines of low hills. Mount Arthur stands magnificent at the head of the valley and it was lined on both sides by hills that had been weathered and worn away by time and erosion, some of them still rugged and beautiful and even after four years I would still get the same feeling when looking at them.

The broad, clear river meandering down the centre is lined with willows and poplars that turn green in the spring and gold in the autumn. The river flats built up with sand and silt are ideal for tobacco and, when the crop is planted, row after row of green plants sway and ripen in the warm summer. In the winter the snow reclaims the mountains and hills and sometimes comes down into the valley.

When I arrived in the valley the farmers appeared happy, they moaned a bit and told us how little money they had, but seemed to enjoy their way of life. The kilns in which they dried their tobacco were small and they loaded the sticks on which they hung the leaf so the hot air could circulate. For the money we were paid, it was a fair day's work for a fair day's pay. However as the seasons passed the farmers built bigger kilns, crammed in twice as much leaf and workers were expected to pick more and more leaf for the same pay.

At first they appeared happy to help one another, but that seemed to change and all they thought about was making money. Alas, most of them had forgotten how to enjoy it. There were only a few farmers who treated their men and women fairly and I had the good fortune to work for one, Cos Newman, D.F.C. and Bar. Being the highest-ranking officer, he took the sword of surrender from the Japanese in Saigon. The workers themselves accepted their lot as the majority of them only worked in the tobacco for the women and the parties and there were plenty of both.

Hundreds of workers pass through the tobacco fields each year and I often wondered what brought me to this little place and, out of all the people who passed through, how did the three of us team up together, Bill, Duff and myself. Was it because we were all on the same wavelength? All of us are different in our natures and not all the same nationality, all of us worked for different farmers, the only time that we were together was on week-ends. Usually we would meet at a party in a batch or down on the riverbank where dozens of workers would be having their own singsong, sitting around a blazing fire, pulling beer out of a keg, singing and playing their guitars. At the end of these parties there would only be the three of us left, blue water dreaming and enjoying the quiet peacefulness.

Christmas arrived and, as the three of us had nowhere special to go, Duff invited Bill and I to spend it with him in his batch. We both knew that his fridge would be full of game – deer, wild pig, rabbits and trout. Duff only went hunting for the table. The three of us sat around an eighteen-gallon keg of beer that took many days before it was emptied, we had allowed for spillage and people dropping in wishing us all the best. Duff confided in us, when he was in his cups, as to why he came to New Zealand. It was an affair of the heart. I seem to remember something about him sprinting across the paddock while shotgun pellets pruned the leaves above his head, and suddenly greener pastures across the Tasman looked inviting. Duff cooked dinner on the day, three big hares, and never have we enjoyed a meal so much. After dinner we all agreed to pool our money and buy a good boat and sail up to the Pacific Islands together. We decided to wait until the end of the season as Duff was growing an acre of weed and he would not be able to sell it until it was graded.

As soon as the picking was over Bill and I put on our packs and started hitch-hiking. We camped anywhere at night to save money as we did not know just how far we would have to travel or how long it would take to find our boat. We went south to Christchurch first, and as we walked down to the harbour I wondered if luck would be with us and we would find our boat quickly. There was a mass of boats of all types and Bill spotted one on a slip a quarter-of-a-mile away and said to me, 'there she is'. As we got closer to her even I, who knew little about boats, could see the strength in her and see the fine shape of her hull. She was a ketch, well built, and both our hearts gave a jump when we were told that she was for sale at a price that we could afford.

After we had talked to a few boat owners who knew the boat, we were advised not to talk to the owner about selling as he was dying slowly of cancer after a long illness and the only thing that meant anything to him was his boat. It had taken him seven years to build it. Bill and I picked up our packs again and headed north. We stopped in the Valley for a day on the way through and when I left I knew that I would not see it again until we found a boat. I said good-bye to all my friends and a girl that I thought a lot of, not an easy task, and I found myself looking back at the mountains around the Valley until they disappeared from view.

I will never forget that we slept on the steps of the church at Nelson the first night. Bill seemed to think it was first class, at least there were plenty of stars and we were closer to our maker. I found the marble too cold and I do not think that either of us slept very much, I heard every hour being struck on the town clock as I lay awake thinking of what I had left behind and what was in front of us. In the morning we were both stiff and cold when we started out for Picton.

After crossing Cook Strait we headed north over much the same ground as I had been before, this time there was more money. Darkness would find us sleeping under the stars and I would say to Bill, "call me when the Cross turns over". During the day we searched any small bay that looked promising and by the time we reached Auckland the decision to go to England and buy a boat looked the best option. We would sail her back to New Zealand.

Bill and I hoped that we could work our passage to England and Duff would join us there after he had sold his tobacco. We went around at least a dozen ships and after hearing what they had to say, we decided to book our passage. The cheapest fare that we could get was ninety-two pounds, and the earliest that we could sail was in two months time. This meant that we would have to live a life we both disliked, living and working in the city.

We went down to the meatworks and when I was asked what job I wanted, I replied, 'The highest-paid one'. I should have been more selective. That day we started work and found it a bit of a shock getting up and working on the midnight shift. Working in the tobacco we had both unloaded kilns where steam was used to soften the leaf, but this did not prepare us for the job in the rendering-down section in the meatworks. When Bill and I entered this section we were enveloped in a white mist of steam. The world that we knew disappeared and for a short time we were lost. It was as if we had both died and were in an in-between state, but there would be no peace for us, no golden light. The heat increased and the stench of death, offal and tallow filled our nostrils. Bill put his head close to mine and said 'Dante's Inferno'. It was as if we were entering some sort of hell world and if he had said to me, "lets get out of here", I would have done so. Moving through the steam we began to make out the rendering-down boilers, were given a rake each and told to pull out the guts, offal, and unborn calves onto bags. When full they would be folded and taken to the presses to squeeze the tallow out. This smell entered our hair and the pores of our skin and we always had plenty of room on the bus taking us home from work as people did not want to be close to us.

Bill and I kept to ourselves and soon got into a routine. We did not go out very much except to get our passports and clearances and were overjoyed when our two months of purgatory were finished. We did manage to save our fare to England during this time. We had received only one letter from Duff, and I was beginning to wonder if he had changed his mind. It was not until he arrived on our doorstep the day before the 'Castel Felice' sailed that we knew there would be three of us.

We boarded the ship in late afternoon. Bill and I carried our packs onboard, Duff had a small case, and not one of us had any good clothes as we were travelling light with as little gear as possible. There was quite a crowd to see the boat sail and we could pick out our Maori friend Tamati from the meatworks in the crowd. He was not allowed onboard as a visitor and I felt sorry for this hard-working man. He owned a boarding house, worked midnight shift and drove his own truck in his spare time. He was a credit to his race. I watched in amazement as a young girl onboard waved happily to her mother on the wharf, her adventure was about to start. Her mum started to cry and begged her daughter not to go and in the end the girl left the ship. Duff was walking around the ship like a stallion that had just been let into the mares' paddock. When the ship left the wharf Bill and I were already down in our cabin which we shared with eight others. I was last in and the top bunk was left for me, so close was my head to the pipes I could hear when the toilet above was flushed and knew if they had been eating peanuts.

The three of us found the trip a little boring, although we enjoyed the meals – especially dinner at night. Our long table had sorted itself out, some left it, others asked to join it. "As above, as below, like attracts like." There was always laughter at our table and any unfinished wine seemed to find its way there. We always enjoyed ourselves at the various ports the ship pulled into. Our wanderings around the back streets and alleys gave us an insight into what life was really like in the different places. The ship was now steaming up the English Channel and soon Southampton would be in sight and the easiest part of our quest over. After travelling many thousands of miles across the oceans it was a sobering thought that our return trip would be in a yacht much smaller than the lifeboats on this ship. Soon the hunt would begin again, somewhere in the backwaters of a little creek or bay the boat we wanted was waiting. All we had to do was find it and another chapter in our lives would start.

Chapter Two

The Boat

Disembarking from the ship took hours with all the queues and holdups. When we finally reached Customs I saw they were going through most of the luggage. However the Customs Officer took one look at the three of us, glanced at our gear, marked it and sent us straight through. Bill's brother Bob and his small son were waiting to meet us, they had not seen each other for five years. We caught the train to the ferry. It was a nice day, much to my surprise as I had expected it to be raining. The trip through the beautiful English countryside delighted me as I had not expected to see so much open country. We caught the ferry to the Isle of Wight and at last arrived at our destination.

I liked Yarmouth when I first saw it because it was small and tidy and the only way I can describe it is to say that it seemed a typical English harbour town. The river Yar runs on the west of the town, from which it gets its name. The town itself has a history dating back many centuries and it was from here that many a small boat voyage started. Bob took us to his little houseboat which was tied up close to the road in the saltings, only a couple of minutes walk from the town. It was quiet and peaceful after all the noise of the ship we had just left. It was great to sit in the twilight and look at the different scenes. On the left were all the masts of the boats and yachts in the harbour standing out against the sky, straight ahead was the town dominated by the church tower and to the right was all open country, my sort of land, with freedom to move without being hemmed in. Just across from the boat the marsh started and stretched out

FOUND — The "Gray Dragon", Hamble River.

in the distance until it was bordered by copse, behind them lay the farm lands stretching beyond to the low-rolling downs.

It was late when we went to bed and by that time all our eyes were burning as none of us had much sleep the night before. We camped on a fifty-foot launch that one of Bill's friends had kindly let us use until we found our own boat. Early next morning we all had breakfast on Bob's boat before we started searching. It was a long, tiring day, but very interesting, as we passed through villages and small towns. The countryside was beautiful and in places looked like some parts of New Zealand. I was very impressed by the way the houses and gardens were kept clean and tidy and I did not see one place that was not looked after.

To travel around the different boatyards was difficult and we seemed to be forever changing buses, trains and ferries. We would have never found our way around without the help of Bob and his wife who came with us and were just as interested in finding a boat as we were. We looked at two, the first one didn't suit us but the second one was just what we were looking for. Bill thought we could go on looking for weeks without finding anything better. We found her in a little broken down yard that at first we were not even going into. The only boat they had to suit us was a Gaff-Yawl and the owner was asking way too much for her – thirteen hundred pounds. It had been laying there for two years and the mast was out of her. When I first looked I was not very impressed with what I saw. She was short in length, only 27 feet, but when we went below and saw the room, the strength of her and the gear we knew she was built for off-shore cruising and was a boat that could take us back to New Zealand. Bill offered a thousand pounds for her and we then had to sweat it out for a day or two to see what happened. In the meantime we decided to try and line up another boat in case the owner would not sell at our price. It was late at night when we got back to Yarmouth and we were all glad to get to bed - our first day's search was over.

The next two days dragged a bit and we spent our time ringing up Yacht Clubs as we found this cheaper than travelling around them. However, we didn't have much luck and did not hear of another boat to suit us. In the end Bob rang the boatyard where the yawl was and when he came dancing out of the phone box I knew the owner would sell. Just then the clock in the old church tower struck four o'clock and as we all sat on the bench at the pier, all quiet now, I knew none of us would forget that moment.

The four of us were up early the next morning and headed off to the bank in London to collect our money which we had sent over from New Zealand. After the inevitable changing from buses, ferries and trains we arrived at Waterloo Station then walked and walked, caught buses and more buses before finally arriving at the Bank of New Zealand. Bill's money was there O.K. but when I asked for mine they could find no trace of it. I spent a very bad fifteen minutes until they eventually found it. We collected the cash in five-pound notes, the whole thirteen hundred pounds, and Bob put it in a little canvas bag that looked like a miniature sail-bag. I think it was the most money he had ever had in his hands, and all day he held on to it like a drowning man to a life-raft because he knew that pay day in London was called 'Snatch Friday'. It took us an hour to find Berkeley Square where Duff had his money and when the four of us walked into the bank I'm sure the guard thought it was a holdup.

We managed to get lost again and wandered around the stone jungle until we found ourselves in Trafalgar Square where we climbed on one of the lions at the foot of Nelson's Column and had our photo taken. From there we headed to Madame Tussaud's Waxworks by way of the underground, which we found was the best way to travel. We stopped for a meal at a small café before going to the waxworks and it was whilst we were lining up for our tickets, we found out how efficient the London C.I.D. could be.

I must admit that we all looked a little worse for wear as we were all dressed in jeans, about a month overdue for a haircut, none of us had shaved as we were starting to grow beards and the bag Bob was carrying looked like something every respectable burglar would have. The first thing I knew was a bloke put his hand on Duff's shoulder and said "What's your name?"

Duff looked him up and down and said "Duff, who are you?"

"Police!" Duff said in his best Australian accent "Yeah". To which the cop replied "Yeah!" and asked us to move out of the queue and along the street so he could question us. Out of the corner of my eye I saw that the same thing was happening to Bill and his brother.

Over against the wall the cop fixed his eyes on me, eyes that said 'go on, just try something', and he snapped out "What's your name?" I gave him one of those 'go to hell' looks and slowly reached into my pocket. His eyes hardened and I presume he thought I was reaching for a gun or a knife because he started to breathe again when he saw my passport. Then the questions started and the only thing he didn't ask me was when I had last cleaned my teeth. We finally managed to convince him that we were not bank robbers and joined the other two. Everything was cleared up and the C.I.D. men explained why they picked us up. It seemed we had been reported by a patrol car as four suspicious characters. While we were having a meal in the café we had an argument about cars and someone, probably the greasy waiter, rang the police and reported we were planning to steal some cars so they moved in on us. I would like to have seen the look on the cop's face when he asked Bob what was in the bag and was told 'thirteen hundred quid'. I could understand why they were so jumpy when I read the afternoon paper and saw that there had been four big robberies that morning.

After the waxworks, which I considered greatly overrated, we went back to Waterloo by the tubes, managing to lose Duff and Bill on the way and did not find them until a few minutes before the train left. The station was crowded as it was knock-off time, hundreds of people were hurrying everywhere and, of course, our train was packed so we had to stand in the corridor. Our conversation was how people could live in these terrible places called cities and travel in the same train to work, day after day, year after year. We had a good example of it a few minutes later when we were arguing whether we should have caught the next train or not. A chap in a bowler hat and suit told us that the next train would have been better and when someone disagreed with him he politely informed them that he should know as he had been travelling on the same train for fifteen years. We could only stare at him as if he was some sort of freak.

I was glad to get back to the peace and quiet of Yarmouth where the only noise was the cry of the seagulls and the sound of the sea. We could not get the boat until Monday and so had a weekend to put in. We went over to Cowes and ordered the charts for our trip as far as Panama, also a second-hand sextant and a grid compass. While we were there we had a look at a seventy-foot schooner, the 'Constellation', owned by a millionairess. She had a crew of six and I would have had to work for a year to pay their wages for a month. All her gear was first class and she had everything on her – even a big, deep-freeze refrigerator.

We were up early Monday and it took us fours hours travelling to reach the yard our boat was in. As soon as we got there we stripped off the cover and got to work. We were like three kids: poking around, pulling things out from here and there and yelling out every time we found something new. The boat was in good condition but there was a lot of cleaning up to do as she hadn't been used for three years and everything on board was suffering from disuse.

Around dinner time the owners arrived from Wales bringing some gear and sails, one set of which was brand new. All the gear was O.K. so we went up to the office and paid one thousand pounds cash for the 'Grey Dragon'.

The boat was built in Brixham by Upham in 1934 of pitch-pine on oak. The length overall was 27.2 feet, beam 8.7 feet and draft 5.25, and had a Thornycroft 9 h.p. motor. She was a roomy boat for her size with plenty of headroom, most of the inside was done in mahogany and the chart table with lockers underneath was a marvellous piece of joinery. All of this work was done by the former owner who only had the use of one arm. He built it on the boat without any previous knowledge of joinery and all of it showed the love he must have had for the boat. His wife told me that when they bought the boat six years before she was a white-faced school-teacher and her husband only had two years to live. The boat brought them closer together during the two years they lived on it, gave her husband back the use of his other arm and, to use her own words, "knocked some of the starch out of me". I found them a very nice couple and they told us that they had had a couple of offers to buy the boat but would not sell, hoping someone like us would come along. They were very pleased we bought her and intended doing such a trip as they didn't want to sell her to some weekend yachtsman. When we said goodbye to them we promised we would send a card and let them know how their little boat was going.

The last few days were fairly hectic, doing the hundred-and-one jobs that have to be done on a small boat. Duff and I were not much help to Bill, as neither of us knew anything about rigging a boat. The main shrouds were old and rather than take a chance Bill renewed them using plough steelwire, splicing them all himself. By the time he was finished he could hardly hold a cup of tea as his hands were so sore. Although we did not want to, there were some jobs we had to let the yard do, such as stepping the mast, because we could not use the winch ourselves. The mast was stepped without any trouble and I put an Aussie two-bob piece under it for good luck, besides we would never be broke while it was there as we could always tell people we had money back on board. With the mast in Bill got to work rigging her but was held up time and time again with gear missing and no eyebolts where there should have been some. Finally the job was done and we towed her off her mud mooring where she had been for so long and put her alongside a M.T.B. We filled our forty-gallon fresh water tank and had to get someone from the yard to free the motor and show Duff how to start it as looking after it was one of his jobs on board. The motor had not been started for three years but much to our satisfaction she started on the first crank.

The M.T.B. we were alongside was war-time built and was nothing but a rotten hulk while the timbers in our boat were as sound as the day they were put in, and when we bored holes for fittings and eyebolts the smell of the resin in the wood was as strong as if the tree was still standing. We were anxious to be in Yarmouth for the weekend so Bob could come onboard and give us a hand with the fitting-out. We worked well into the night, bending the sails on and getting ready to leave. We decided to motor out to the mouth of the river and then sail her under main and jib as there were no fittings for the staysail. We paid the bill which came to sixteen quid, money we had to spend but could not really afford, and I am afraid by the time we left we had a lot less than we had hoped.

When we left the yard nearly all the workers came down to see the old boat go and wish us luck. They all had a good laugh when we tried to start the motor with the petrol off and finally we were away and motored the three miles to the river mouth through a lane of small boats and yachts. I saw more yachts on this Hamble River than I saw in the whole of New Zealand. The motor ran well all the way although at first she smoked and smelt terrible. I felt sure it was going to blow up any moment and it didn't give Duff any peace until it settled down and ran properly. Once the motor was stopped and the sail up, the boat seemed to really come to life, just moving along with only the sound of the water against her sides. We had to tack all the way to Yarmouth and she did not sail very fast as the bottom was foul and we were towing our dinghy which was half full of water. She was heavy on the helm without the staysail but when Bill rigged it temporarily it performed much better and was easier on the tiller. It was the first time I had touched a tiller under sail and I enjoyed it greatly, but realised I would probably be sick of it by the time our trip was finished.

Bill brought it into Yarmouth with the motor and it was the first time he had not sailed a boat into harbour. I could understand the feeling he had for small boats and sail. Bill and his brother Bob had bought, repaired and sold many yachts that had been neglected, and some whose owners sadly never returned after the war. Eventually they were able to buy a real sailing yacht, a twenty-seven-foot William Fife design double ender which they sailed in the Solent and around the unspoilt, beautiful coast of England. Bill's next love was the 'Dasia', a Cornish lugger built in 1898, which he rebuilt below and could hardly wait to finish work and get back to her. He could stand and just look at her as a man might look at a woman he loved, and at night he would feel peace and security in the cabin listening to the hiss of the small stove while his meal was cooking. She would come alive as the tide gently lifted her out of the mud until she was swinging free and tugging her ropes as if eager to be away and out in the open sea.

As soon as we tied up in harbour Bob was down at the boat. While we had been away he had been busy making enquiries and lining up gear for the trip. When we left it would be the third time he had stood on the wharf and watched his brother leave on such a trip, the hard part being that it is the life he and his wife would like to lead. Like so many others they do not like the conventional way of life, and his dream was that one day he and his brother would get a forty-footer between them and live and sail on her. When we arrived in England Bob, his wife and small son were waiting for a sailing date to migrate to New Zealand and the sunshine, but they got a letter saying they could not migrate as his wife had a spot on the lung.

The following day, September 3rd, 1961, we took old 'Needle Nose' out for a trial sail. Once we got all the gear ready we lost track of the time

Alongside the Quay, Yarmouth

and days and dates did not matter much. We all had been busy at our different jobs: Bill building lockers for our supplies, Duff with his palm and needle and me with a paint brush. Slowly the boat was beginning to look as though she was ready to go and things were forming a pattern, just like a jigsaw puzzle with only a few pieces left. The weather had been beautiful, hot and sunny, and it required an effort to work on such wonderful days, it would have been much easier to lay in the sun on the deck.

One of the main jobs finished was the bottom. We put the boat against the quay wall on the hard and waited until the tide was dropping, then we went over the side with scrubbers and scrapers and gave the bottom a thorough scrub followed by a good coat of antifouling. The boat had a well-shaped hull and I was pleased to hear the old sailors standing on the wall looking at her say that we had 'a good ship there'. I was glad when the job was finished and we were back out in the harbour away from the wall and people who stood and stared down into the cabin from daylight to dark. Duff was a bit put out when he opened his eyes in the morning and saw three heads peering down at him, and I forgot where we were when changing my pants and looked up to find a group of interested spectators copping a good eyeful.

When we left the quay wall quite a mob was there as we had just hoisted our brand-new New Zealand flag and I think most of them thought we were heading for parts unknown instead of just out in the harbour. Duff started the engine and we let go the bow-and-stern lines. Bill took the tiller and put her into gear, the boat moved about six feet and sprang back again. For the next fifteen minutes we pushed, shoved, tried pulling it along the quay, but always it sprang back. Bill kept saying "I can't understand it, its as if we are still tied on". I thought that perhaps we were still on the bottom in a bit of a channel.

The spectators were enjoying every bit of it when one of them came over to Bill and said quietly, "Do you want to get away from here?"

Bill said, "Yes, but she doesn't seem to want to leave".

The bloke pointed up, the only place none of us had thought to look, and there we were with the mast still tied to a rail on the quay! I took off down below so no-one could see my red face. Duff looked around at the laughing mob and yelled out: "Quick, get that bloody flag down and hoist the British one." With that he dropped the boat into gear and we took off across the harbour, none of us daring to look back.

I don't think it was Bill's day because after having a few quiet drinks at the pub he stepped into the dinghy to go back to the boat when a roller caught him off balance and tipped the dinghy over. The only remark I made was to tell him it was a good chance to test his watch and see whether or not it was waterproof, but you could hear Duff laughing half-a-mile away. Most of Bill's old friends helped us fit the boat out, lending tools and gear, and Allan, one of his old sailing mates, rigged the boat out with emergency battery lighting and refused to accept anything for it. His mates on the 'Constellation' gave us a lot of useful gear and we were indebted to all the people who helped make our trip possible.

Another week passed and finally the sextant we had been waiting for arrived from Scotland after three phone calls. The following day we planned to sail around to Cowes and pick up our stores, deciding that all being well we would sail with the tide on a Wednesday afternoon. We took old 'Needle Nose' out for a few sails while we were waiting. She sailed stiff with an easy motion, which was the way we wanted it, and although not very fast compared with the modern yachts, owing to her cruising lines, we thought she would get us to our destination O.K.

The annual dinner terminating the end of the racing season was held in Yarmouth on the weekend, and never have I seen so many yachts in one place at the same time. The harbour was so packed in fact that many boats had to anchor outside. From late afternoon to dark they came in, one after another, from all along the coast, and even some from across the Channel flying the quarantine flag. Each day was the same and the best part of the day here in harbour was just to sit on deck at twilight and watch the boats come in one after another like pigeons seeking shelter for the night. It seemed that in England more and more people were going back to the sea to escape from the crowds and the traffic. Many of the boats were manned by women who sailed and rowed better than some of the men. It was nothing to see whole families on small boats with the young children, some just starting to walk, with their life jackets and safety ropes on, playing around quite at home.

Three reporters and a photographer came on board during the week. One of them already knew Bill as he had written a story when Bill left twice before. They got a story and took some photographs and promised they would not print anything before we left. Another boat, a sixteen-tonner, left Dover a couple of days previously bound for New Zealand with two men on board, and it seemed probable we would run into them somewhere. We heard there were no less than forty yachts waiting in the Canaries for the right weather to cross the Atlantic.

We could not sail up to Cowes as there was no wind, it was dead calm in the Solent, and we motored all the way. It took us all afternoon to

Last drink before leaving England.

order our stores and fix everything up and we had to wait until the next day for our bonded stores and clearance from Customs. Our bonded stores consisted of ten pounds of tobacco and two cases of whiskey at 11 shillings a bottle. Not one drop of this was to be touched as we bought it as an investment to sell and barter for food when our money ran out. All our stores amounted to sixty pounds, making quite a big dent in our money. Counting what we had left Bill led easily with fifty quid, Duff came in second with thirty and I was a bad last with fifteen. The bigger the battle the greater the challenge.

Customs came on board and sealed our bonded stores and wished us luck. At last we were ready, the barograph was on board and there were no more holdups. However the weather blew up all night, gales all along the coast and in the bay, and it was raining and blowing like hell when we left Cowes to go back to Yarmouth. The boat ahead of us had a spitfire jib and was reefed well down. It was too good an opportunity not to try our boat out so we went under full sail to see what the old girl could do. She really sailed for a while with her gunwale hove down to the water's edge and once or twice she dipped the bowsprit. I really enjoyed it, sitting out in the cockpit with my feet braced against the other seat getting the feel of her as she raced through the water with the rain hissing down in my face. Only once did I go below to have a smoke and Duff took the tiller. After a while the wind eased off, the rain stopped and it was more enjoyable. The boat behaved splendidly and we were all pleased with her, but we realised we could expect much worse conditions before reaching the Canaries. We dropped the sails off Yarmouth and took the boat into harbour with the motor. Bill went ashore to phone the Met. Office for a three-day forecast, which they got from a weather ship stationed in the Atlantic, and it seemed we would not be able to sail for at least three days.

Chapter Three

Yarmouth to Vigo (Spain)

Monday, 18th September, 1961, was a beautiful day, the wind had veered around to the north-east, blowing moderate to fresh and we could leave at last. Three days of these winds would take us clear of the Channel and give us sea room in case of a gale. I spent the last few days collecting minerals along the coast, and one day we hired a car and drove around the island to see the sights. The weather was starting to get a little cool and we would be glad to get into warmer waters. At 12 o'clock we took the boat alongside the wall and put our fresh stores aboard, filled the water tank and took on twenty-two gallons of petrol. A few friends were there to bid us farewell, so we gave them a whiskey and cracked the bottle of rum Cos Newman had given us a long time ago in New Zealand just for this occasion. The three of us all had a good stiff drink without any water. Just as we thought Bob wasn't going to make it he arrived on his bike so we said our goodbyes and promised to meet in New Zealand. Duff started the engine, Bill took the tiller and I let go the bow-line, something I had waited four years to do. Cameras seemed to come from everywhere, but we were moving out into the Solent by then where there was work to do, sails to be hoisted, gear to be stowed and the dinghy to be lashed down on the cabin top. We had started perhaps one of the greatest adventures of our lives.

We didn't make very good time going up the Solent as we had the tide against us and didn't pass the Needles Lighthouse until 1600 hours. I watched Bill staring back at it with that faraway look in his blue eyes, no

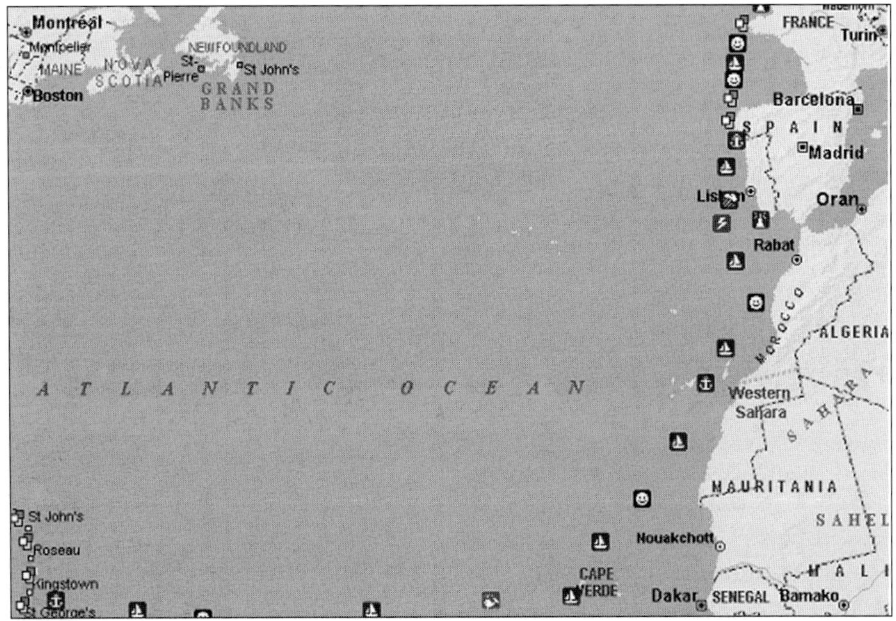

England to Bay of Biscay, Vigo, Canary Islands, West Indies.

doubt remembering when his father was the Chief Officer at the Needles Signal Station. For a treat Bill would be allowed to look through the very large telescope at passing ships and yachts, and so began his passion for the sea and sailing. We had a good six hours of ebb tide to help us. Out in the Channel we were met by a cross sea left over from the gales earlier in the week. Our boat was soon turned into a strange world of constant erratic motion where to forget, for an instant, to hold on would send you crashing back clutching wildly for support. The hardest part of this motion is that the mind and body are tensed nearly all the time and cannot relax.

Duff was the first to feel the effects of the sea as he was down below in the galley trying to lash the pressure cooker full of good Queensland stew on to the stove. His head came out of the hatchway and I found myself looking at the strangest colour I had ever seen, a cross between a green and a white. On deck he let go a string of abuse that lasted for about five minutes then went strangely quiet. For the next two hours he made those terrible noises that sounded as if he had swallowed a tin of bicarbonate of soda. Bill felt the motion a bit after being so long away from the sea and had to keep coming up for fresh air. The sea treated me kindly, not bothering me at all; in fact I could still sit back and suck on my old pipe. All of us managed to eat a good meal, but we ate it out in the cockpit.

Bill streamed the log, Duff set his inevitable fishing-line and we settled down to our first night at sea with Duff taking the first watch. The winds were fickle and changed twice during the night, once during Bill's middle watch and again during mine. Just as I was trying to work out the muddle I sighted a lighthouse that should not have been there. It turned out to be the Channel Islands and we were ten miles off course. After tracking down just how we came to be so far off course it seemed some clumsy clot had kicked the compass and altered the grid setting. It turned out to be me!

In the morning I cooked a good breakfast but we were all showing signs of little or no sleep, with red-rimmed eyes that felt as though someone had thrown a shovel full of hot coals in them. While we were having breakfast a forty-foot ketch came up under sail and motor and said they were looking for England. They had been in a fog for five days. We gave them a course for the Needles and they went on their way. I wondered how the 'Four Square' was getting on, a thirty-footer with two men on board that left Yarmouth a day ahead of us bound for the Canaries.

Our run for the first twenty-four hours was eighty-one miles and the sea and sky were a depressing grey all the time. Duff looked at his line in the morning and found only half of it left – it didn't look as if we would be eating much fish. I had been trying to pick up the shipping forecast on my forty-quid radio I bought in New Zealand, but although I could get twenty stations I couldn't get the one I wanted. I would have very much liked to bend it over the head of the bloke who sold it to me. The wind was against us and we would have to do a lot of extra miles before we cleared the Channel.

At night there were ships all around us, all we had to do was light the sails up with a torch and they would keep well clear. A couple came right alongside and lit us up with their searchlights to make sure what we were. At night I found it easier to steer by a star in the rigging instead of the compass, and it was better to tie a rope around the tiller and let the boat sail itself as it knew more about it than I did. We were not sure where we were as we hadn't been able to get a fix on a light for a while, the last one being what we presumed to be the Eddystone light. However, the light list differed from the chart and I was not sure in my mind that it was in reality the Eddystone light.

The tack we made must have taken us out a bit into the Atlantic because we sighted the Ouessant lighthouse at 1600 hours and everyone brightened up considerably. Duff had his first smoke for four days and Bill laughed for the first time since leaving Yarmouth. He had been feeling pretty crook with bladder trouble and was in a lot of pain. Now that we were close to the Ouessant we were sighting ships again, passing one after another. It had turned out to be a nice day, what was left of it, and Duff was having one of his novel washes over the side while I held onto his legs. He blew and snorted, making just as much noise as the pod of small whales who had been swimming around the boat further back.

The motor started without any trouble and we cleared the channel at last after four days. We motored twenty miles out in the Bay of Biscay to clear the Ouessant and were welcomed by a beautiful sunset, the first of many we would see. It had a background of piercing blue and light green, roofed with wool-like clouds of red, a ceiling of deep velvet that no real velvet could ever match, and lit with rays of gold and yellow and tinged with pink. Long after the sun had gone the pink remained silhouetting the clouds against the horizon, then the moon came up and lit the water with its silvery path. Just to sit there and watch it made me forget the loss of sleep, the burning eyes and the damp bed and clothes. It was just as well we used the motor as the wind dropped and the log registered only seven miles all night.

We were now a hundred-and-fifty miles out in the Bay of Biscay, just halfway to Cape Finisterre on the north-west tip of Spain. Yesterday was a beautiful day with a warm sun and we were able to dry out most of the bedding. The sea was gentle with a light south-east wind that took us steadily on our course south-west, not very fast but pleasant sailing. Bill took down the heavy staysail and put up the light canvas to help us along. The wind had dropped out overnight and we logged less than one knot for three hours. Although we were unhappy about using the motor, we were anxious to clear the northern part of the Bay, so we started it up and were pushed along at four knots an hour on half throttle.

The motor had been plugging along steadily hour after hour and we stopped it for a while to let it cool down, and to refuel, oil and grease it. Duff cooked a good breakfast that would take a lot of beating. The wind sprang up for a while from the west-north-west but died quickly, so once again we started the motor. The sea was calm and covered with a heavy fog that cut visibility down to a mile at the most. With the sea so calm it was easy to see any marine life and we sighted a ten-foot shark swimming close to the boat, but it didn't take a crack at Duff's fishing line.

Although no fish had yet been caught he did pull a gallon tin of heavy grease out of the water that had not even been damaged. This morning we had a visit from a sparrow who rested a while on the mast and then flew off – so far from land.

We are all sleeping better now and getting used to the boat and her ways. Soon all the noise will be commonplace and the mind and body will adapt itself to this life as if it had known no other. It is hard to say when the day really begins on a small boat at sea. You could say with first light, but then the day and the night blend as one, only the darkness makes a difference because then your senses have to be more alert. I think the most important thing on a small boat is sleep and that is one of the hardest things to do. On a boat the size of the 'Grey Dragon' there is very little room for good bunks and what there are take up a lot of room. Our boat is laid out down below for two people with a double bunk in the cabin. Duff tries to sleep on one half of it and the other half is used for stowing stores. Bill tries to sleep up forward, where the motion is the worst, in a pipe cot so short that no-one else but him could sleep there. I have the best bunk on the boat – the quarter berth. It is like sleeping in a coffin with the end knocked out, at least you cannot be thrown out of it.

At 10.55 p.m. Bill finished his three-hour watch and it was my turn for the middle one, 11 to 2. He put his head through the hatch and called "John, 11 o'clock". I hadn't been asleep, just dozing, and his voice came from a long way off. You know you have to get up but your mind tries to stop you from coming awake so your body can get the rest it needs. Finally you overcome it and drag yourself out of the bunk and slide across the chart table. You grip hard to stop yourself from being flung off, blink your eyes and shake your head, trying to clear it, while at the same time tasting the sour taste in your mouth. Your eyes clear and in the half light you watch the deckhead for a moment, watch its crazy roll, then try and find the deck with your feet. Just as you stand upright, before you get your balance, you are thrown bodily across the cabin, clutch wildly for the upright on the double bunk, miss and hit your head on it. You now grab hold of it, steady yourself with the other hand on the chart table, swearing all the time. You are wide awake now, the knock on the head helped, so you put your coat on. It takes a long while because with the swaying you can't seem to find the armholes. Finally you're ready and look up through the open hatchway at the dull, overcast sky and the smell of salt and damp are in your nostrils.

You look at Bill. He looks like a man who has been on a six day binge, hair that hasn't been combed for three days and probably won't be for another week is all over his face, his red beard matted and encrusted with salt, his blue eyes red-rimmed and sore from lack of sleep and staring at the compass. He looks as if he had aged ten years in very short time. You climb the ladder out into the cockpit and take the tiller from him, squinting to see the luminous lines on the compass.

You sit down on a wet cushion feeling a bit sore as you are chafed from wearing wet clothes. You watch as Bill stumbles below and lights the light over the chart table. He stops there for a while working out the course and position before he goes up forward. He doesn't sleep because no-one could sleep up there unless he could sleep on a buckjumper – besides, the worry of navigation is on his shoulders. For the next three hours you sit out there alone. You are not yet used to the steering and still find it hard. Every now and then a wave will send its spray over you and you swear aloud because you were thinking of the Valley back in New Zealand and more pleasant things. The water brings you back to reality, to the pitching and tossing, and you stare into the black night. The first two hours pass quickly but the last one drags a bit and you sing softly to yourself waiting until its time to call Duff.

It is 1.55 a.m. and the wind is easing up a bit. You stand and stretch your cramped limbs and peer down into the dark cabin. Just for a few seconds the light catches Duff in his bunk, the canvas sides bulging as they hold him in against the roll. You wonder if he is awake and move across the cockpit. For a brief moment you were thinking of Duff and not the boom and it swings across and catches you a blow right on the ear. There is another string of curses and you thank God you've got a hard head. You stumble through the hatchway down the swaying ladder into the cabin, but even before you get half-way Duff speaks, swings his legs out of the bunk and sits there holding his head in his hands.

Back you go to the tiller to put her back on course. Down in the cabin you hear Duff moaning and swearing about not being able to sleep, having the same trouble trying to put his clothes on and think with a dulled brain. He seems to take a long time and you keep looking down trying to see what he is doing. Finally he pushes himself up through the hatchway, takes the tiller and for the next three hours he will be alone with his thoughts. Down in the cabin you get rid of your clothes as fast as the motion will allow, then climb up on the chart table, holding on while trying to find the opening of the sleeping bag with your feet. It's damp, but right then you could not care less, all you want to do is get into it.

Finally you manage and push and wriggle down until you feel your feet hard against the petrol tank, roll over onto your back, shut your eyes and tell yourself to sleep. The deck is only a foot from your head, you open your eyes and watch it moving with your body rolling in unison. Six inches from your ear part of the ocean surges past, the noise it makes reminds you that the shell of the boat is so thin. It is impossible to sleep on your back, so you roll over on your side drawing your knees up until they are pressed hard against the bridge deck, feet hard against the inside of the cockpit and your back pressed against the side of the boat with the three ribs there digging into your spine. You don't move much in that position but the noise robs you of sleep for a while. You feel the boat rise and crash down in a trough, feel the timbers shudder. Just as she is rising a wave crashes into her side like a blow from a giant fist, she shakes from stem to stern and you wonder how she can stand such blows without caving in. You sleep for a while, how long you do not know. On deck it sounds like all hell has broken loose and you lie there listening to the noise.

It takes a while to realise that the wind has dropped and different noises take over. The sails flap as if they are tearing themselves to shreds, the boom crashing backwards and forwards is the worst. It sounds as if the boat is breaking up. Every block creaks and the sound of rope rubbing is everywhere. Just above my head the lee backstays sound as if one of the first Australians is there, rattling his leg chains. Down below the water sloshes in the bilge and the noises coming from the galley are many and varied, every pot seems to rattle and every dish slide. Somehow sleep claims me and when I sleep I snore, good and loud, and Duff reckons that it is the worst sound of them all.

You feel yourself waking up and try to fight against it. It seems as though you have only been asleep five minutes and again you wonder what has woken you. The wind has risen and spray is coming down through the open cockpit right on your face. You force your eyes to open and find that it is light, in fact it is around 8 a.m., and it's up to you to cook breakfast. You look over at the galley, watch the kettle, which is tied on to the stove, swinging to and fro on gimbals, and think what a picnic you are going to have. You go through the same trouble getting out of bed and getting dressed, look through the hatchway at the helmsman but his back is turned and his head down watching the compass.

You feel as though you have a terrific hangover and have to think of something two or three times before your hands respond and do it. You find the metho and prime the stove, then go on deck, lean over the side and swill your face. You stand for a minute, blinking your stinging eyes and wonder what it will feel like to have a shower again and get the clammy feel of salt off your skin. Suddenly you remember the stove and jump down below. You hear the helmsman say good morning and grunt a reply on the way down but you are too late, the metho has burnt out and you have to prime the stove again. You sit there and watch the flame, running your tongue over your teeth and remember that you haven't cleaned them for a couple of days.

You fill the kettle and tie it back on the stove, forgetting that you have to take it off again to light up. You go over to the food cupboard to get some bacon. It looks as if everything was just thrown in and you sort through the stuff looking for what you want with one hand while holding on with the other. Having made it back to the galley without losing anything you wedge the stuff anywhere to stop it from sliding, in the sink, in the plastic bucket, everywhere you look is full and tied down. You light the stove and it flames and smokes for a bit before settling down and burning properly. You light the other burner and put the bacon on, but the old string is burnt through and you have to go across the cabin to get some more. You're not half-way before the pan follows you, throwing bacon all over the floor. By this time you've resigned yourself to the situation, swear just once, get the string, throw the bacon back in the pan and lash it onto the stove.

As soon as the kettle boils you take it off and start making toast. There is no way to tie it on and it comes sliding off as many times as you take your eyes off it to do something else. With the toast finished you start on the eggs, poaching is best because it doesn't matter if more water gets splashed about. While you're waiting for them to cook you start buttering the toast, wedging yourself so you can use two hands. Half-way through, the boat gives an extra, big roll, the toast flies everywhere and you make a grab for the butter dish and save it. However, the knife goes down in the bilge to join many other things that have found their way there, all the water is out of the pan and an egg sits neatly in the middle of the mat.

You get the dishes ready and yell out to Duff to get out of the sack. You serve out a portion for Bill and hand it through the hatchway where he eats it, one hand still on the tiller. Duff says good morning then starts abusing me for snoring too loud. I hand him his breakfast and tell him to eat it or wear it, so he goes up in the cockpit to eat. He is still not used to the motion and down below in the cabin is more nauseating. I put the kettle back on and join them. The food is almost cold and Duff and I eat quickly with one eye looking for spray. Down below I go again, judging the pitching and rolling, and manage to make the cocoa with the loss of only the sugar which flies out from between my feet. The three of us sit in the cockpit sipping our cocoa which makes us feel much better. The cooking finished I am willing to leave the fun of washing-up to someone else. Duff takes over the tiller from Bill so the washing-up falls to him.

With breakfast over and Duff on watch there is only one place to go, back to the sack. It is no different now that it's daytime, but with the light you try and hunt down all the drips and leaks, but give up in the end, lay back and doze until it is once again time for you to go on watch. You are roused by someone jumping around in the cabin, look over and see Bill, pants caught around his ankles as he's trying to kick them off, jumping around as if he was in a sack race. He has no other clothes on except a woollen cap jammed on his head and stuck under the side of it are three pieces of paper. From this you know two things, he is the outdoor type and he is going to answer a call of nature, instead of using the toilet up forward, and coming out feeling relieved but as if he had just gone over Niagara Falls in a barrel, he is going up top to face the elements.

You know he can expect a comment from the helmsman, it will vary depending whether or not he was behind the door when they were handed out! He goes up the ladder and stops, one foot on deck and one on the ladder ready to dive back inside should a big wave be coming. His skin is covered in goosebumps as soon as the cold wind hits him, but he steps out on deck like a peacock showing off his feathers. He can easily feel which way the wind is blowing and moves along the lee side holding onto the guardrail until he reaches the mast stays, then, waiting his chance, climbs out board. The knuckles stand out white on his hands and the veins swell in his arms as he holds on tight with every roll of the boat trying to fling him into the sea. Every wave tries to sweep him off, failing to but wetting him with their spray. All the time the helmsman watches idly, careful to note the amount of strain in the eyes and the amount of tremble in the legs as there will be comments to pass later. The job done the hardest part now comes because to use the paper you only have one hand to hang on with, this you do with precision timing, watching the waves like a master mariner. The battle won he steps back on board and hopes that he doesn't have to go through that again for at least twenty-four hours.

You find it is time once again for your turn at the tiller. It is better up there in daylight as you can see the waves coming and meet them with more confidence. There are always things floating in the sea to arouse your interest and while steering you might watch the antics of a seagull for an hour or so before tiring of it. The hours pass quickly enough and Duff puts his head out of the cabin, has a look at the weather, then comes up dragging what looks like half the galley and you know he is going to get the stew ready. It takes a lot to fill the big pressure cooker and as he peels vegetables we talk of old times.

It is about 4 o'clock in the afternoon when Bill gets up and looks out at the grey sky, checking the rigging and sails to see that everything is alright, then goes down to the chart table to work out our position. His brow is furrowed with worry as he works it out as he has not yet gained confidence in his navigation. Satisfied, but not sure, he comes up and takes over the tiller and I go down below, get my head down and listen to Duff fussing around in the galley like a broody hen with chickens. The smell of the stew cooking makes me hungry and I hope it won't be too long before it's ready. However, I know it will take a while yet as there are spices and thickening to be added, plus all sorts of secret ingredients which he mixes like a chemist and refuses to disclose to us.

It is close to sundown when Duff's voice rings out proclaiming that the stew is ready and if I don't get up and eat it he will throw it out of the scuttle. I slide out of my bunk and join Bill at the tiller. Duff passes half the kitchen up again followed by toast and stew dished out in deep-sided pannikins. It's hot and tastes marvellous but Duff dips his spoon in, tries it, grimaces and, as always, states that there is something lacking although everything but the kitchen sink is in it. He looks around the heavens as if searching for a clue then shouts, "Condiments, that's what its lacking", puts his head down and eats like a man who hasn't seen food for a week. I go below and make the cocoa, pass it up and the three of us sit in the cockpit sipping it slowly so it will last. There is no sunset to watch so we sit and talk of many things until darkness comes.

At 8 o'clock I take over the first watch while Bill and Duff go below and wedge themselves into their bunks. Alone on deck I try to learn the ways of the sea and sail, listening to the sails shake as the boat veers up into the wind and move the helm to put the sails to sleep again. Every now and again I stand up in the cockpit to stretch my cramped legs, my eyes trying to pierce the black night for any sight of land, ears straining for the sound of breaking waves and nose to windward to catch that foreign smell of land. Down in the cabin, among all the different noises,

Duff moans and calls out in his fitful sleep. Looking at my watch I see that it is time to wake him, lash the tiller and go below. As I touch him he sits up frightened, still thinking of the dream he was having, calls out to make sure it's me, and when I speak he sighs and sits there trying to get used to the motion before getting up. Back at the tiller I find that she has held her course and wait for Duff, then the long day will be over.

Sunday, 25th, and we have been at sea a week. No wind last night and the sea so calm it looks like a big lake. We used the motor all night but in the morning the wind sprang up from the E.N.E. and looks as if it might last this time. Bill rigged the buoy hook up as a staysail boom, boomed the sail right out and in combination with the mainsail it pushed us along. It was fine and sunny all day and in the late afternoon the wind was blowing strong and steady from the N.E. moving us along at six knots. No pitching and tossing now, just a good, steady roll, under spinnaker she could really sail. Just as well the wind came when it did because we have used almost as much petrol as we can afford to, as the remainder must be kept in case of emergencies.

During the night the wind became stronger and we dropped the mizzen and reefed the mainsail for the first time. It was too rough to sleep and Bill didn't call me for my watch but stayed at the helm for six hours. In the morning we took down the staysail, reefed the main some more and just ran under it. The seas were the biggest I had seen so far, about 12 feet. So far the boat has not shipped a solid wave or run with her gunnels under, but she is taking on a fair bit of spray. Heavy rain squalls last most of the day with the sky overcast and black, rolling thunder and flashing lightning creating a wild scene. We should sight the lighthouse on Cape Finisterre soon, but it will be hard to see in this weather.

We have run the distance on the log, 350 miles and no sight of land. The seas have dropped a bit so it could mean that we are in the lee of it. Bill rolled more sail down on the main and hoisted the jib. The miles covered in that 24 hours were 130. During the afternoon, in a strong wind, Duff gybed her but luckily no damage was done. While I was at the tiller a 12-inch squid came on board and landed under my arm – I don't know who got the biggest fright! When I touched it the deck became covered with its brown, oil-like fluid staining the green paintwork.

Early in the night the wind dropped and the sea soon calmed. All that night and the next day we were becalmed. The hot, sunny day gave us a good chance to dry all our clothes and air out the boat. There is no sight of land but it must be close. Duff saw a bat flying around the mast just on daybreak and there was a dragonfly on the rigging. Land birds have been landing on board, resting a while, preening and cleaning their feathers before carrying on with their journey. One little yellow-jack flew on board, hopped around poking into everything and then walked the length of the deck, head moving right and left like an admiral's inspection. He looked dissatisfied, jumped up on Duff's sleeping bag, relieved himself and flew off.

We put the fishing-line over the side baited with the squid, but still no fish. The water was so clear we could see the bait down to 150 feet. During the day we all went for a swim, diving into deep blue water, turning and looking up at the keel of the boat, every detail of her powerful hull standing out clearly. We were careful not to swim too far away as we were unsure of sharks and also would have been in an awkward position if the sails suddenly filled and the 'Grey Dragon' sailed off and left us all in the water. The calm gave us a chance to clean the boat and we soon had it shipshape again.

Just on dark a light wind sprang up and by next morning we were on our way, punching into a moderate breeze. At dawn, whilst I was at the helm, I sighted a steamer cutting our course. As it drew closer Bill could hear the thunder of its motors below and came up and joined me in the cockpit. So far all the steamers had altered course when they sighted us, but not this one, and at 500 yards we turned down-wind to avoid being cut in half. She passed us at 200 yards, the wake throwing us about everywhere. There was too much noise for them to hear me so the most I could do were some rude gestures directed at the bridge.

During the afternoon the wind grew stronger and we took down the staysail and reefed in the main. Big seas were making the boat uncomfortable and Bill was still unable to take a sight due to rain and poor visibility. Late afternoon we sighted a lighthouse but were unable to identify it and so tacked out to sea. We sighted a Spanish fishing-boat a few miles out and hoisted the V flag which means "we require assistance", so that we could verify our position, but they were trawling and continued on. We sailed out from the coast into the shipping lane, with the wind getting stronger and the barograph going down fast.

Early in the night the wind swung around favourably so we set all sails and drove her hard into head seas, spray reaching high in the rigging. After a while we found we were pressing too hard and had to reduce canvas. There were ships everywhere and we had to keep a good lookout. We sighted two lighthouses but could only find one of them on the chart and wanted the second one for verification, so we still could not be sure where we were. Towards morning we had to reef down some more and just on dawn signalled 'V' to a small coaster to find out our position. She circled us and came in close but, seeing we were alright, sailed off before we had a chance to talk with them. It was a wild night and none of us turned in, the two off watch sitting in the cabin smoking and trying to work out the lights, and the one on watch huddled in the cockpit cringeing and getting soaked with every wave.

Soon after the coaster left us we reefed right down. What a job it was: in the half-light with the rain pouring down, the wind howling through the rigging, trying to stand on the heaving deck and haul on halyards that bit into water-soaked hands and the crest of waves breaking all over us. The boat had taken a terrific pounding and the words of the old seamen of Yarmouth came back to me: "The boat will take as much as the men!" Duff, who in a moment of weakness had volunteered to do all the cooking, managed to make a cup of cocoa. We hove to under reefed main and staysail, lashed the tiller and went below. It is amazing how the motion of the boat ceases when hove to, just a gentle rise and fall and down below in the cabin all the noise is shut out. If we could have lit our little wood stove we would not have asked for anything more. Just sitting there drinking cocoa and having a smoke made us all realise how sleepy we were. It was hard to keep my eyes open and I found myself going to sleep, cigarette in one hand and the mug in the other, and by mutual consent we all turned in. Being so close to land, and in the shipping lane, perhaps we should not have, but we had to sleep, and sleep we did for six hours, leaving the boat and fate to look after us. It was still raining when I woke up but the sea was down and there were fishing-boats trawling all around us. I got back into my sodden clothes and woke up the other two. We decided to start the motor, go alongside a fishing-boat and find out our position. I was a little sick of sailing around not knowing where we were, as our last good fix was on the coast of France.

It was tricky to come alongside the fishing-boat close enough to be heard as there was a large swell running, but Bill took the tiller and managed it alright. It was all to no avail, as we could not understand his Spanish and he could not understand our English, so I decided to jump aboard her and take the chart with me. Bill circled and came in close enough for me to jump across without any trouble. There were only two on board, the skipper and a young lad. I was taken to the wheelhouse where we laid out the chart. I don't think he had ever seen one before, he seemed lost and his brow wrinkled as he ran his thick finger over the chart until he found Cape Finisterre. Then he got excited and his face broke into a smile as he tapped his finger on the chart and the pantomine began as he followed the coast down. The words that came out of his mouth meant nothing to me but his face and gestures told me all I wanted to know. His fingers told me how far and I followed them down the chart to Vigo, our destination, but he was not sure and searched the names of the towns and rivers inland. I held my breath as I watched him and let go a sigh when he thumped the table and nodded his head pointing to Vigo. He took my arm and led me over to the compass, pointing to the east and holding up his hands for fifteen. To make sure I went all over it again using much the same gestures. There was no doubt now, Vigo was to the east and very near. We both relaxed then and the skipper pulled out a packet of Spanish cigarettes and offered me one but I told him I did not smoke. As he lit up I looked out at our boat standing off, rolling in the swells. She looked good from here but very small compared with the fishing-boat. I thought how pleased the boys would be when I told them where we were, after eight days of sailing without a fix we had hove to right outside of Vigo. Call it what you like, but it certainly makes me think, as we were not even sure that we were still in the Bay of Biscay.

Bill brought the boat in but it was rolling too much and he circled for another try. The skipper asked me where I was from and where I was going and when I told him he looked at me and the boat, looked sad and shook his head. Then he told me the Spanish words for all the compass points plus a few others he probably thought we might need. He took me into the wheelhouse and showed me his big wireless and echo sounder which he turned on and showed me the fish they were following. I felt a bit sorry for the fish as it doesn't give them much of a chance. He pulled out a battered mug which had seen years of use and filled it full of white wine from a five-gallon jar at his feet

The wine was good, but not the best on an empty stomach and I had to drink it fast as Bill was bringing the boat up again. I could feel it running down my beard. Bill had to take the boat around for another try and I had plenty of time to finish it off. I turned and thanked the skipper. Our rough hands met in a strong handshake and our eyes studied each other for a moment taking in our old jerseys, then our eyes met. Both of us had too many crows' feet around them and our smiles were a language we both understood. He spoke rapidly in Spanish for a moment, I guess he was wishing me luck, and we went down on deck and watched the boat come around.

This was Bill's third try and if I didn't have the charts with me I would have dived over the side and swam to her. As the boat got closer I got ready to jump and as she drew level I jumped, knowing she was too far out, and managed to catch our guardrail with my left hand. I swung my head around quickly to see how close the fishing-boat was but she swung back after just touching our stern, twisting and snapping the bolt in the log bracket. The look on the lad's face was one I laughed about for the rest of the day and I couldn't resist giving him the thumbs-up sign as I was towed along in the water up to my waist. For the next couple of days Duff called me Captain Blood. I just called myself lucky.

With a parting wave to the fishermen we headed east, set all sails, left the motor running to help us along, and in a couple of miles sighted land. It was late in the day when we steered for the middle of the two islands marking the entrance to Vigo. Down below the boys were trimming beards, cleaning shoes and humming to themselves. Then it was my turn. Duff took the tiller and Bill went forward to try and sleep. What gear they had was all laid out and I thought back to the time when I was in the Navy and it seemed just the same, the old excitement of a new port was still there. When I dug my shoes out from the bottom of my locker I found they had grown whiskers about an inch long but they came off without any trouble. When my gear was all ready I went up and took over from Duff.

As we went through the narrow passage the breaking waves sent their spray high up on the rocks. On one side was a small light and on the other an iron cross high up. Once through the passage the water calmed and we moved through yellow foam into the magnificent big bay of Vigo. Fishing-boats were everywhere. Outside the entrance the big boats trawled their nets and all along the shores of the bay more fishermen rowed their boats and spread their nets. Boat after boat passed us heading out towards a black sky that promised a dirty night, but the crews didn't seem worried and waved and called a greeting as they passed. It took us two hours to get from the entrance to the port. We stopped our engine out from the yacht club just 50 yards from the quay and dropped the anchor.

Chapter Four

Vigo

It was dark when we rowed ashore to have that hot shower we had been talking about for the past week. All along the quay were more fishermen with their fine-tipped long rods fishing for small squid, and they greeted us when we landed. At first the ground heaved and rolled like an earthquake but settled down quickly and we made a beeline for the showers only to find that they were cold. However, we got the salt off and headed up town to a cheap café where we had a Spanish meal and

Drying out in Vigo.

a bottle of wine. When we finished we headed back to the boat and sleep, none of us moving before noon the next day.

Bill and Duff went ashore in the afternoon to buy food and some parts to fix the log. It was nearly dark when they got back and all Duff could talk about was the women he had seen ashore and declared he would like to spend the rest of his life in Vigo. I wondered what he would say when we got to Tahiti! It didn't take long for both of them to get out the shaving gear and shave off their beards. Bill claimed his did not suit him and Duff made no bones about it, he was going out after the local talent.

The first couple of days we were all busy doing little jobs that had to be done on the boat; drying our gear and catching up with our washing. We went ashore every night for a meal, and tried a different café each time. It did not matter that we could not speak Spanish. We just got a toothpick and tried a bit of everything, until we found something we liked, and some of the things we ate – Ugh!

I did not see anything of Vigo and ventured no further than a quarter-of-a-mile from the boat. The town had big, wide, paved streets, and was kept quite clean. The Spanish people struck me as being easy going, very friendly and went out of their way to help us. When Bill dropped seven pounds in pesetas in the street, a little boy came up, gave it back and ran away before Bill could thank him. Because we only mixed with the poor, I can only talk about them. Most of the people are very poor, and earn less than two pounds a week. For a meal ashore, with a bottle of white wine, it cost us about three shillings.

Meat was very expensive and only the rich could afford to buy it. We priced some bacon and it cost ten shillings a pound, so we did not eat any meat while we were in port. We had a lot of fun buying vegetables, especially when we tried to describe a potato. We tried half-a-dozen different names, but it was no good and we could not see one to point to, so Duff started to dig for spuds in the floor of the shop, going through the motions of putting the fork into the ground and turning it over. The shop was crowded and every eye followed the imaginary fork into the ground, and watched him shake the dirt off it. Their eyes never left the spot for a moment, and I wondered if they thought we were digging for treasure.

When I thought that the digging had gone on long enough, I bent down and picked up an imaginary potato, cleaned it and then started to peel it. Immediately, the uproar started, with everyone arguing what it was supposed to be. While all this noise was going on, I spotted a box of them pushed away under the counter, went over and held one up. Everyone went silent, then those who were right had big smiles on their faces and nodded their heads to those who were wrong. They all waited to see if there was something else that we did not know, and I think to their disappointment we got on alright after the potato.

A Norwegian forty-foot fishing-boat came into the harbour and tied up alongside the wall. She was headed down south to the Canaries with only a man and his son on board. Never have I seen such a strong ship as her, all her timbers were fastened with wooden plugs and there was not a nail or screw in her. We went ashore and had a meal together and a talk. He was an interesting chap to listen to and was headed for the Galapagos Islands to fish, so it was possible we could run into him again.

We all went back on board our different boats about eleven o'clock, that is all except for Duff. He set off up the road with a moist look in his eyes, whistling to himself, and headed for the nearest brothel to try out the Spanish senoritas to see if they had as much fire in them as he had been told. Back on board Bill and I speculated for a while as to how he was getting on, then turned in. We were both awakened from a deep sleep about three o'clock in the morning by a loud crash that brought me out of my bunk like a rocket. All I could think of was that the anchor had dragged and that we were being thrown against the quay wall. On deck, I saw that we were still off the wall and was looking around for the boat that hit us when I heard a groan from the bottom of the cockpit. I looked down to see that Romeo had returned, so drunk that he could not scratch himself let alone get out of the cockpit. Judging from his language as I watched him trying to get up with the tiller holding him down, he thought that someone had a foot in his back.

It seemed he had met up with a mob of sailors off a Spanish warship, went drinking with them, forgot all about women and spent two quid in a place where wine can be bought for just over two pence a glass. He then invited half the Spanish navy on board. No doubt they wondered where they would all fit, because none of them turned up the next day, or perhaps they all had a hangover like Duff. Making his way back to the boat he had got lost, finally found his way to the quay, leant over to look for the dinghy and fell head first in the water, then climbed aboard the dinghy, half filling it with water, and rowed it out to the boat just as it was. The crash we heard was him hitting the bottom of the cockpit, and back in the cabin he kept us awake telling us all about it. The language he used made the Spanish fishermen on the quay bless themselves many times.

The next day being Sunday we did not go anywhere. Bill and Duff made some chafing gear and I kept plugging away at the typewriter. The Spanish senoritas were out in full force, parading up and down in their best finery, but all of them had chaperones, which Duff says does not give a man a fair chance. On the Monday we got the forecast we had been waiting for and got our passports back from the Yacht Club. That was the only thing we had to do while we were there as no-one came on board, told us where to anchor, or bothered us at all. Bill and Duff went off to fill the petrol cans and, by the price of it, we will not be using the motor too much. We all went ashore again; Duff to buy some more fishing gear and a guitar, Bill to get a spear gun, flippers and goggles, and I went to the market to buy the fresh food. Siesta time came and all the shops closed for two hours, so we had to wait until three-thirty to finish our shopping, then filled the water tank, pulled away from the wall and headed out to sea watched by some solemn-faced Spaniards on the quay.

Chapter Five

Vigo to Las Palmas (Canary Islands)

It was eight o'clock by the time we were outside the entrance and the wind we were hoping for was not there. We were still there at eight o'clock the next morning, when the wind came up against us and did not change favourably until twelve the next day. We did a hundred miles with this wind before it dropped and becalmed us, three miles off the coast just off Cape Mondago. Both topping lifts on the mizzen and main masts chafed through and had to be renewed. Finally we lowered the main to stop the chafe a bit. It was a good chance to catch up with some sleep, while Duff was still trying to outsmart the fish.

Ever since England, he had been trying to catch a fish; spending hours getting his gear ready and making elaborate lures. He tried spinners, wobblers and fish, painstakingly cut out of old meat tins, complete with fins and tail, with red feathers pinched out of a hat tied to the belly. All types of different hooks were tried, some carefully disguised with red-and-white plastic, others just left bare, trailing behind some lure. All sorts of sinkers had been made. Odd bits of lead ballast out of the bilge mysteriously disappeared to turn up flattened out and rolled in sinker form. Once, the boat was covered with odd bits of line and lashings. Now they had all gone, and appeared only when the knots showed on his fishing line. The fifty-foot burgee halyard disappeared when Duff decided a longer line was needed to clear the wake.

While I was trying to sleep he hauled his line in over the gunnels and it sounded as though he was pulling the hawser of a destroyer on board. He is using what you would call fresh bait now; herrings bought from the fish market of Vigo, which he had salted so that they would keep. Just when I was in a deep sleep, he catches a fish. His yells bring both Bill and me on deck. On the way up I am thinking of a big piece of fish for tea, but lose my appetite when I see the six-inch fish he is proudly swinging on the end of his line. He fishes for another couple of hours without any luck, and when we are about to leave he hauls his line in only to find a smaller one on it. It does not matter to him about the size, for he can still say that it was off the village of Quiaios, near Cape Mondago on the coast of Spain that he caught the first fish for six hundred miles.

In the late afternoon, we started the motor and ran it until we had cleared the Cape. It was dark by the time we cleared it and found the winds against us. Heavy rain and squalls most of the night meant we had to reef the main. I had the morning watch and it pelted down with rain all the time. It was one of those pitch-black nights when you hope you don't find yourself in the middle of a fishing fleet and do. The next morning was squally and wet with strong gusts of wind and at one stage we had no time to reef and had to drop the mainsail in a hurry. I was called on deck out of a warm sleeping bag to get the sail down, with no time to put my pants on. I went on deck in the rain to find Duff huddled over the tiller and Bill hanging in mid-air, trying to get the sail down. Between us we managed it; clawing and heaving the wet canvas in and lashing it to the boom. Not a very nice job when you are bare arsed to the wind. In the afternoon, the wind swung around to a good sailing breeze and the warm sun came out.

A good wind all night pushed us along the coast towards Cape Vincent, only one-hundred-and-fifty miles away. No trouble with navigation as we had been picking up the lighthouses as we went. It was good sailing, but right in the shipping lane, and ships seem to flock around these lighthouses like flies around a dead horse. I had the middle watch and the lights of Lisbon were on our port hand. As I watched the lights of a steamer coming towards me, I made a stupid mistake that almost cost us the boat. As she drew closer to me, I decided to pass to windward of her thinking that her course was parallel, and instead of steering by the compass I steered by her lights in the rigging. I did not realise that I was heading the boat into the wind so much, until I lost the steerage way.

With our boat dead in the water, I grabbed the torch, flashing it on the sails and towards the oncoming steamer, and watched as this massive hulk of steel bore down on us. For what seemed an eternity, the knife-edge bow pointed straight at me, the luminous bow-wave glowing in the dark. I shouted down to Bill to get on deck quick, not that there was anything he could do, but on deck he would have a better chance. Duff, I thought, would hear the shout and come up. I had to shout a couple of times before Bill heard me and came on deck like a shot. He stood there trying to clear his sleep-filled eyes, no doubt hoping that he was still in his bunk and that it was all a bad dream. There was nothing we could do. The helm was up and we stood there like two interested spectators, waiting for the climax. My jaw was clenched tight and my hand gripped the now useless tiller. I felt no fear, only anger at myself, and then slowly the steamer began to turn. Her stern swung towards us like a black wall, and then slid past, her powerful engines thudding and her wake boiling. I do not know what they said or thought on the bridge, but I deserved every bit of it and if it was not for their fast reactions when they saw my light come on almost under their bows, we would have had a midnight swim off Lisbon.

Down below, Duff was still in his bunk, trying to work out if he was dreaming or not. With the danger past and our boat back on course, I waited to hear what Bill would say. I knew that it would not be much as he is not a man given to the use of strong language, but I consider that he made the understatement of the year when, as he passed me on his way back to his bunk, he said, "That was close!" It was two cigarettes later before my heart resumed its normal pace. The rest of my watch passed without any trouble, and when I saw a steamer coming five miles away, the torch was close to my hand.

The sky was grey in the morning, the winds stronger and the sea playful. By that I mean a sea that catches you off balance and throws you across the cabin, seems to delight in throwing the kettle off the stove, and if you are on watch and roll a smoke, just as you are about to light it, a cupful of water comes over and wets it. The winds grew stronger around midday and we took the jib in, reefed the main and staysail in a squall, and it was Duff's turn to get caught with his pants down. The boat was taking on a lot of water, solid stuff, and everything was wet again. The wind was slowly pushing us on to a lee shore. We were only twenty miles out and needed seventy miles to clear land. The sea was rough and even I am not smoking so many cigarettes, so in the end we turned around and headed back up the coast to Lisbon.

The last time Bill was in these waters was aboard an eighty-year-old ex pilot cutter called 'Norderson'. These same blustery Portuguese trade winds hit them on their way to Madeira and in the strong winds and large seas the old boat began to open up and take on water. A Very light was used to bring a vessel alongside and when given their position after explaining their problem, they made the decision to slow the boat down and reduce the water coming in. They headed for the Canary Islands, which they reached in three days and were towed in to port by a small freighter. They proved the old saying true that "a few frightened men with buckets can move a lot of water". They bailed for three days to keep their boat afloat.

We had only gone six miles when the wind swung around to the north, and as we could clear land with it, we turned around and headed back along the coast towards Cape Vincent. I will be glad when we get clear of land and the shipping lanes and get out in the safety of the open seas. As we headed down along the coast, the wind eased off a little, but the large seas were rolling in and taking us on the beam, throwing us about something awful.

I must take my hat off to Duff. Ever since he took over as lord of the galley doing all the cooking, no matter how rough or how much we have been thrown around, he has always managed to cook us a hot meal. Down in the galley with these seas running, he is getting ready to put on some soup. Finding out that there is no metho to prime the stove with he is standing spread-legged, bracing himself against the roll, while his two hands are occupied trying to fill a small jar out of a two gallon can of metho. One of the bigger waves picks up the boat and bodily throws it sideways. There is a crash as he is thrown onto the stove, smashing it off its gimbals, his head ending up in the shelf with the pots and pans, his right hand still holding the can of metho upright to stop it from spilling. He gets up, makes a joke about wearing a saucepan as a hat, finds his jar, fills it, and lights the stove.

The motion is a bit too erratic to lash the pot of soup on the stove and he stands there holding it with one hand until it is hot enough to eat. Outside, the helmsman calls the seas. As a bad one comes up he calls "Watch it", and the soup comes off the stove until it has passed, and then back on the stove it goes until the next bad wave. In more favourable seas Duff is able to cook better, and what he does to a tin of bully beef is amazing. He mixes the dough, cuts up meat, onions and whatever he has, adds spices and herbs, covers it all up like a big pancake and cooks it in the pan. When one side is cooked, he stands in the centre of the cabin, holding on with one hand, calls our attention, then flips it up in the air. Up the mystery bag goes, almost to the deck-head, then it turns a lazy circle and lands back in the pan. I am still waiting for the day when the boat will roll and it will land at his feet. No doubt he will just scoop it up off the floor, put it back in the pan and try again.

Later that night, when the seas had settled a little, we put the miles behind us with a good sailing breeze and at midday the next day were off Cape Vincent lighthouse on the south-west tip of Portugal. With a light wind we set our course for the Canaries, leaving Europe and the bad weather behind. We all caught up on sleep that was badly needed. That night during Bill's watch he saw his first ghost. He had lashed the helm and gone down below to make a cup of coffee. He checked to see if Duff or myself were awake, and believing we were both asleep bent down and started to light the stove. I slid out of my bunk onto the chart table and stepped over Bill, unseen and unheard, out into the cockpit Wearing very little I found the wind cool so put on a long, gabardine coat that used to belong to his father while I had a look around for any ships. With the stove alight Bill stood up, blinded by the flame, and looked out to see a fourth person onboard, the coat flapping in the breeze. Slowly he approached, apprehension and fear etched on his face. I wondered what the hell was going on and moved away until my back was hard against the mizzen mast. It was not until his face was inches from mine that he shouted "YOU!" and started to breathe again. When he told us the story Duff and I laid Dad Corbett's ghost to rest with a smile, while we both pondered whether we would have had the guts to put our faces inches from what we thought was a ghost.

The next day was one that we had been waiting for since we left Yarmouth: hot and sunny with a good sailing breeze. Duff cleaned up the boat as if there was going to be an inspection, and at midday we decided to go over the side and have a wash. Both of us are still a bit wary of sharks, I climbed over the bowsprit down onto the bobstay, and, hanging onto it, let myself into the water, wrapping my legs around the bow. I did not stop in long, the force of the boat moving through the water made it hard to hold on.

Duff was a bit uncertain about going in but, after calling him all sorts of names and assuring him that there was not a shark around for miles, a statement I hoped was right, he dropped in the water, only to come out so fast that the hairs on his legs were not even wet, saying "What if there is a shark under the keel?" The same thought had passed through my mind a few minutes earlier, but I dropped back in the water to show him that there wasn't, and stopped in about two seconds longer than him. I then decided to go over the stern and hold onto a rope and get towed along while Duff took a photo from the bow, getting some of the boat in too. Over the stern it was better being towed along, after you got the thoughts of sharks and the rope breaking out of your mind, and the force of the boat through the water surged you along on top of the water. After he had taken the photo I came back on board and he decided that he would have a go.

Instead of lowering himself over the stern, Duff jumped holding onto the loop in the end with about twelve feet of slack rope. He disappeared about two fathoms down and came up at the end of the rope with a jerk that almost tore his arm out of the socket. He looked like a walrus coming up to breathe, and had a look of amazement on his face. Just as he opened his mouth to shout something, he was towed under and swallowed a good share of the ocean, came up looking like a half-drowned rat, pulled himself painfully along the rope, and hauled himself back on board. When I said "Good, hey?", his reply was, "Bloody marvellous, bloody marvellous!" as he tried to extract the salt water from his lungs.

The next day was another beautiful day, with the north-east prevailing winds behind us billowing our sails and pushing us along at a steady pace. I found it a bit hard to steer with the wind right aft and gybed her when the preventer-stay chafed through but, luckily, no damage was done. There was a bit more chafe in the rigging and Bill had to go up the mast twice with it swinging from side to side, doing its best to throw him off, but he confirmed Darwin's theory and clung there gripping with his fingers and toes like a monkey. Instead of going right to the African coast and picking up a light to get our bearings, we altered course at midday, eighty miles off the coast, and headed straight for the Canaries. Bill has been taking latitude sights every day and is gaining more confidence in his navigation.

With us getting into the hot weather the dress of the day is birthday suits, and it is just as well, too, as nearly all our clothes are worn out. Our faded jeans we treasured the most were first to go. The knees suddenly poked through, then the hole caught on a bolt, and soon the leg was flapping. First one, then the other, then the backsides wear through after many hours of sitting in the cockpit. After the flapping legs are caught and torn off the jeans become shorts, but still they are not thrown away. They remind you of too many things. Our only set of yellow oilskins, that kept us a little dry when we first started out, no longer look like oilskins. The knee-length coat has been torn and trimmed so much that it is now the size of a small vest. The pants have only one leg left, the other cut off at the thigh. All the shirts and jumpers have the sleeves missing or big holes worn in them from rubbing on the side of the cockpit while at the tiller. It is hard to muster enough clothes between us so we can all go ashore together, and if anyone could see us dressed in what we have, they would think that we had sailed from the North Pole and been at sea six months.

For the next three days the winds kept pushing us along, sometimes the motion so smooth it was hard to believe we were not in harbour. At night, we sometimes reefed the mainsail to make the boat better to handle. We sighted the Island of Alegranza dead on our course at eight o'clock in the morning, and Bill was as happy as a kid told to go home from school at lunchtime. Duff and I missed out on our bit of fun as usually, when a place or a light does not turn up when it should, we are full of helpful suggestions. Duff usually suggests putting the names in a hat and pulling one out. When he receives a blank stare he walks around the deck talking like a Yank, stating that he always wanted to try a hot dog. I usually tell him that my grandmother favoured the pin system and offer him a big, shiny needle, but he always refuses.

With the latitude sight, Bill found that the current was pushing us along ahead of the log about ten miles a day, enough to get you into trouble if you did not take it into consideration. We sighted our first flying-fish around the Island, and Duff was up on deck all hours of the night with a torch, looking for breakfast. We are almost out of fresh vegetables, though we only eat two meals a day, and will have to take on a hell of a lot for a long passage. Friday the fourteenth was good sailing all night but with the cross seas we have had since we left Cape Vincent. Towards morning, the wind swung around until we were sailing by the lee. We sighted land at midday. It was very hard to see, as there was haze all around the horizon.

We were expecting to see the Grand Canary Island up ahead, but only sighted a faint outline of the small island at the top of it. It was off our port beam about twenty five miles away and disappeared in the haze soon after our sighting. It would be very easy to miss these islands as we did not see any part of the big island until close to sundown, and then only the tops showed through the clouds. The current that Bill had allowed for did not push us as far south as he had hoped, probably owing to the deflection off or around Fuerteventura Island. In the afternoon, when the visibility was about ten miles, we could hear the engine of a ship but could not see her. The only thing that it could have been was a submarine.

The winds were light in the afternoon, and we were still a way off at sundown, the setting sun silhouetting for about five minutes the island of Tenerife, fifty miles away with its twelve-thousand-foot mountain. It then disappeared with the sun as magically as it had appeared. It was twelve o'clock at night when we dropped the anchor behind the breakwater in Las Palmas and the 'Grey Dragon' had one thousand seven hundred miles of water under her keel from Yarmouth and twenty-two days of sailing. Our best run was from Cape Vincent to Las Palmas, six hundred and sixty-five miles in six-and-a-half days.

Chapter Six

Canary Islands

It was a great relief to be in the still waters of the harbour and know that we could sleep the rest of the night without any cares. Leaving the boat swinging slowly around on the anchor chain, we all went down in the cabin and sat without speaking, listening to the hissing of the stove as the water heated for coffee. All of us had a feeling of great satisfaction. We were not long in turning in and I slept on deck, as we had heard that there was a lot of thieving in the harbour. I don't think I would have heard much because, when I finally got to sleep, I did not wake up until the sun burnt me out around ten the next morning.

It took me a while to get to sleep, as there was a fun fair not too far away. When I was just getting used to this noise, all hell seemed to break loose ashore. I sat up listening to the tramp of hundreds of feet on the cobbled streets and the sound of many voices chanting and singing, followed by loud explosions that sounded like bombs and rifle-fire. I thought, "Just our bloody luck to land here in the middle of a revolution", until I looked up in the sky and saw the fireworks, then the bombs became skyrockets and the rifle-fire became just ordinary crackers. I did not find out until next day that it was one of the big feast days for the Spanish, but even all this noise was not enough to keep me awake for much longer.

I was amazed when Bill told me that he and his friends had spent a year living here aboard the 'Norderson' after her leaks were repaired. They were diving on wrecks along the coast, bringing up copper pipes and fittings from the engine rooms. One wreck they dived on for some time was the steam sailing ship 'Effonsoi'. She lay in one hundred feet of water and had gold bullion aboard, most of which was retrieved by suit divers. Bill said they had tried to blast their way in to where they believed the rest of the gold was, but it became too dangerous and two of his friends started to get the bends due to spending too much time at that depth.

I was not very impressed with the place when I had a look around in the morning. The water in the harbour was so thick with oil that it looked as if you could walk on it, and all my hopes of spear-fishing faded quickly. The town itself looked much the same as anywhere: crowded and too many buildings. The mountain slopes around the town were barren and void of any vegetation. No wonder the dogs on the fishing-boats close by howled all the time, they would find it hard to cock their legs. We soon found that we had anchored too close to the fishing fleet and had to put up with the stink of fish all the time. We did not bother to move our anchorage until one night, while we were having tea, the boat dragged the anchor and took a trip around the harbour, probably looking for a better place.

We had to start the motor to stop the boat from taking some paint off a black Spanish yacht whose owner was getting very excited, and in the end we anchored in the middle of all the yachts in the harbour. There were yachts from all over the world and we found out that we had missed an Australian one by two days. Bill went ashore the first day to make enquiries about canvas for our spinnakers, timber for our booms and to repair the gaff jaws. Had he known how long it was going to take he would have given up the first day.

It does not pay to be in a hurry in Spain, for with the Spanish there is always Manana; tomorrow, tomorrow. It took us over a week to get a sailmaker on board to measure up for the sails, then his price was much too high and we had to start all over again. Bill almost wore out a pair of shoes by the time he found another sailmaker and got him on board with his bits of string to measure up. Then he did not like taking work from the first sailmaker, so we had to pay the first one two hundred pesetas for nothing before the second one would take the job. Back then to buy the canvas and rope, only to find that the price has risen, so you do a round of the shops looking for cheaper canvas, and in the end finish up going back to the first shop and buying it. Shopping in Spain is very complicated, especially if you cannot speak the language and have very little money.

Bill and Duff went ashore the second night for a quiet drink and found that the price of things had risen to three times as much, including the women, much to Duff's disappointment. My first trip ashore was to the beach for a swim which was only a five minute walk through the town. There the water is clear and the long reef only a few hundred yards from the shore is ideal for spear-fishing. The beach itself is over a mile long and covered with golden sand. The buildings on the foreshore with their bright colours blend with the colours of the tents and umbrellas of the people who come from all over the world to winter here.

We soon settled into harbour life. Every morning Duff would take his bag, row across to the quay and then make his way up the streets and alleys to the market, where he would bargain for our food for the day. The locals soon got to know him and would greet him every morning showing him where to buy the cheapest fish. I had heard so much about this market that I went up to have a look for myself. Not only could you buy food there but almost everything was for sale, from secondhand shoes to paint by the gallon. All of the paint and the tinned stuff comes off the ships that stop in the harbour. As you walk among the stalls you see tinned milk from Holland and the best of English tinned meat and fruit. On the counters are fresh butter from Norway and New Zealand plus cured hams and bacon for those who have the money to buy them. Much of this tinned stuff, especially biscuits, have the stamp on them "For cabin use only". Quite a lot of this stuff can be bought far cheaper here than the country from which they originated.

It was on one of his trips to the market that Duff found a fourth member for the crew. He arrived back on board with a bag of spuds and onions in one hand, and a canary complete with cage in the other. Never has a canary been looked after so well. The small seed bins in the cage were always full, and stuck in the wire around the cage would be figs, pieces of banana and cuttle-fish. For days we waited for it to start whistling, but in vain. In fact, we spent so much time sitting around the cage whistling to it that there was very little work done. In the end, back to the market it went, cage and all, where we were told that the hen bird does not sing. After much arguing and a few more pesetas we arrived back on board with a fine-looking bird; not a pure canary judging by his speckled head and the odd grey feather here and there, but he did manage to make a noise occasionally when he got his head out of the feed bin for a moment. Most of the time between eating, he spent in front of the mirror, hanging on his cage preening his feathers or taking a bath in the water bowl. The only thing we worried about was how he would take to the sea and if he would be a good sailor.

The boat had taken on a better appearance with all the work we have been able to do while waiting for the sails. Duff was doing most of the cooking and looking after the paint work and mahogany down below. Bill was doing most of the rigging, shaping and planning the spinnakers, booms and cleats, varnishing the mast and booms, and any wire splicing that was needed. I looked after all the paint work on deck and varnish on the cabin, cockpit and hatches. By doing a little bit every day, we gradually got the boat shipshape. In the middle of this work, a squadron of British frigates arrived in the harbour on a 'showing the flag' visit. They overdid this a bit by flying flags ten feet long and six feet wide.

In no time at all, whalers and skiffs were sailing around to the different yachts in the harbour, inviting everybody aboard for a drink in the evening. First, a midshipman came on board to tell us that the captain would like our company on board his ship at six-thirty, then a couple of marines came along. We gave them a drink of whiskey, but I think they were a little dubious when the water was poured from a blackened old pot. When they left we told them the best yachts to go to; that is the ones with the most drink on board. It is always hard to get any work done in harbour, owing to Harbour Rot. This affects the people, not the boats, and work that can usually be done in a day takes a week.

That day there was no work done, and shirts, dresses and suits that hadn't been worn for months came out of lockers to be aired on deck. There were a few on the smaller boats like us that did not have any suits, and we spent part of the day ironing some creases in our khakis on the chart table with a navigation book, and as there was only one tie between the three of us, we all went open-necked.

The ship we were invited aboard was the outer one of the three and, as we went aboard, we tried not to look too self-conscious, as the officer of the watch and quartermaster sprang to attention and saluted us. We were shown across the ships by the Duty Officer, and when I saw the cut of the crowd I slowed my steps a bit. All the officers were in full whites and medals, and the town dignitaries were accompanied by their elegantly dressed wives and daughters. The officers of the Spanish army, navy and air force were there with their ribbons, medals and yards of gold braid; and standing in one conspicuous group, which we made a beeline for, were all the small boat crews; the wanderers of the sea. They all looked out of place with their untrimmed beards and creased suits, a few women standing out among the many with their legs, arms and faces burnt mahogany brown. There were a few world wanderers who get around any way they can and who own nothing. It was one of these, dressed in faded jeans, who was stopped by the stiff-shirted British Consul and told to get off the ship as it was his party, only to be pushed past with the reply, "Balls to you. I am invited on the other ship." After that, he did not try to stop anyone.

It was quite a good evening, with all the boy-seamen acting as waiters keeping the double rums up to us as fast as we could drink them. The only time they fell down on their job was when Duff, feeling quite happy by then, collared them all in a bunch to give them the address of the whorehouses ashore. This little group was only broken up when the captain, with an empty glass, stood stern-faced behind them listening to Duff telling the attentive audience how to ask in Spanish for what every sailor should know is the international language.

There were only a few officers who came over and mixed with our group. Most of them would say a few words with a very affected accent, look down their nose at us and get away as fast as possible. To these I happily told that the last time I was on a ship the same as these was as a

Farm in volcano crater, Canary Island mountain village, Canary Islands.

seaman, and the only time I was on the quarterdeck was to lift my cap on some charge. This made them move away from me even faster. We got on very well with an Australian midshipman doing his training on the ship. When he first came up he also talked with an affected accent, but after talking with Duff and me for a while, soon dropped it and spoke in the slow, throaty drawl of an Australian, throwing in a few oaths I'll bet he never used in the wardroom. We were all in a very good mood when at last the bar was closed and we made our way across the ships and down the gangway. No doubt the quartermasters thought the same as I used to, as they saluted and watched us weave our way along the bay.

We had a visit from the sailmaker who, instead of telling us that the sails were ready, informed us he needed more canvas. The six days that he spoke of had gone into ten, and still one sail was not finished. How long will it take? Perhaps another six days, maybe ten? So I packed my kit-bag, put on my heavy boots and headed back up into the mountains to have a look around. It cost me only two pence in the bus from the port to Las Palmas, and by sheer luck I got out at the right place to catch a bus to take me along the road to where I wanted to go, the Caldera de Bandama. It was a small bus, like a Volkswagen, with only a few on board, mostly farmers' wives who had come to town to do some shopping. They were all dressed in the rough, black dresses that most of them wear.

Leaving the town behind, the winding road climbs into the foothills, and on these barren slopes the poorer people of the town live in caves that are no more than holes in the volcanic rock. The road follows high above the winding path of what once would have been a fair-size-river, but now in its bed and along both sides of its banks of volcanic ash and cinders, bananas are grown in small blocks, surrounded by high, cement walls. The rich, black soil for these blocks is brought down by truck from the high mountain slopes too steep to farm. Most of the houses are made of brick and cement and the high, open-topped water tanks are made of the same material. These are the only means of irrigation, and are filled up with the scanty rainfall in the winter months.

The art of the stonemason is not lost here, and huge piles of hewn stone are cut down in the valley where the rock is suitable. Further away from the coast the hills have a small scrub growing on them, similar to saltbush, and prickly pear is plentiful, its red spiny fruit edible. All along the road tall gum-trees are growing, and some places remind me very much of parts of Australia. After passing through a few small villages where, as always, the church is the most impressive building, I left the bus, shouldered my pack and left the road. Soon I was well out in the country, walking along lanes with whitewashed walls and hedges of red, purple and orange bougainvillea.

The only people I met on the road were an old woman and her granddaughter who were doing the weekly washing by a small shady tree close to the road. As I passed by, the old one asked me the time; one of the few phrases that I knew in Spanish. When I told her, she thanked me and offered the only thing she had: a drink of cool, clear water. She, too, was dressed in black and was very old, her body bent and stooped, so that it was hard for her to walk. As she drew closer with the shining dish of water, I saw that although her hair was white and her face lined with the passing summers, her eyes were still amazingly clear. The last I saw of them was when I was high in the hills, and looked down to see two tiny figures walking over the rough ground towards a farmhouse; the old one in the lead, and the granddaughter following, carrying with perfect balance a large tin of water on her head.

Around me now, as far as the eye could see, the valleys and the steep hillsides were covered in grapevines. The season had finished and the workers were moving among them preparing for the next. Not one piece of land that could be farmed was wasted. Close to the crest of a very steep hill I found myself looking down into what I had come to see, the Caldera de Bandama, a huge, extinct volcano.

Across the lips of this volcano it was over a mile wide, and almost perpendicular walls formed a gigantic cone that sloped slightly toward the bottom, which was dead flat. Here was a farm of many acres and in the centre of the ploughed fields were the farm buildings, all painted white. As I stood looking down at this unique sight I had the good luck to see how they took some of their provisions down. First they loaded them onto a sleigh, then one man pulled it over the edge of the crater and ran ahead of it with the speed of an Olympic runner. He was as sure-footed as a goat and kept just ahead of it all the way until he was obscured by the rising dust three-quarters of the way down. After that, I do not know what happened to him or the sleigh.

Moving up to the crest of the mountain, I was able to look across the low hills and valleys, the patch-like flat land and, in the distance, the sea. Making my way back to the main road again, I tried to go to a town well inland but was told I had to go back to Las Palmas to catch the bus which only went there once a day. I tried three of four buses to get to the next town but was unsuccessful as it was siesta time, so I could only shrug my shoulders and head back to the port and the boat. After not wearing boots for a few months my feet were not the best, and I was glad to throw the boots into the bottom of my locker where they will stay for the rest of the trip.

Our Norwegian friend from Vigo had been in the harbour over a week, and he and his son also wanted to have a look inland. I was very glad to go with them, as among the many languages he spoke, Spanish was one of his best. After a couple of days painting on board, the three of us took our sleeping bags and very little else, arriving at the bus depot a few minutes before the bus was due to leave. Pandemonium reigned as sweating farmers, dressed in their old patched suits, complete with a knife stuck in the belt, tugged and strained to load their town-bought goods on the rack on top of the bus. There were bundles and baskets of all shapes and sizes. Many were the large, cane-bound bottles of wine that were stowed with much care on top. Large crates of live chickens were helped up by many hands, until at last we were ready to go. The bus started with a loud bang, shook like a small boat in a heavy sea and, with a lurch and a grinding of gears, we were away right on time. Quite a few of the passengers were asleep before the conductor, who looked as if he had not had a shave for a fortnight and smelt as if he had not had a bath for at least twice that long, could collect the tickets. The road followed much the same valley that I had been up before it branched off and climbed steadily higher and higher. All along the winding road were planted gums and pine trees, and it was not until we were far inland that the dry, barren hills began to show the first faint sign of greenness.

We passed through many villages and stopped at some of them to let the engine cool down, as the steam and boiling water hissed out a good three feet in the air. It was not until we reached the plateau that the green really showed and the small farms on the rich soil were packed with all kinds of vegetables. Because all these farms are small, they are well cared for and must yield a terrific crop. Along the edges, bamboo is grown and the green tips are used for fodder for the animals. Across the other side of the plateau, deep down in the gorge, were the first cave dwellings to be seen. The bus then travelled through some dry, rugged country of volcanic ash and rock, passing close by old craters, long dead, that helped to carve the geology of this island.

A few miles from our destination, the bus topped a rise, the radiator boiling like mad, and stretched out before us, down in the valleys and ridges were miles and miles of the small, terraced farms belonging to the

Mountain village, Canary Islands.

people who lived in caves, just as their ancestors, the Berbers from Africa, did many hundreds of years ago. The bus arrived at our destination, Artenara, sounding like a steam engine, and we got away before the unloading began. Around us, the rugged mountain tops reached high up in the sky and along the narrow mountain paths came the sure-footed donkeys and their riders to get the supplies for the villages where no roads run.

After looking around the area we made our way back along the road to where one of the largest valleys lay. It was almost dark when we reached it and we decided to go into one of the small farmhouses close by and buy some cheese to go with the bread we had got in the village. The farmer was sitting out in front of the house in the twilight and, after greeting us, asked if he could help us. As soon as we asked about the cheese, he called out to his daughters, who brought out three different types and a knife, so we could try some of it before we bought. It was very fine cheese and we settled on a block made of cows milk instead of the goat, and bought a quarter of it at a third of the price you would pay in town. He then asked if we would like some hot water and while this was being boiled, told us how the cheese was made, while his wife stood close by spinning wool onto a wooden spindle. The milk is separated by using the natural intestines of a calf or a kid. These are taken out and dried, and when placed in milk, continue to do the same work, the skimmed milk running out of a groove under the cheese, leaving the rest to harden in the wooden mould. When the water boiled, the farmer invited us to eat in his house. He lit the lamp and it was only then that I saw his wife was blind.

I was very interested to have a look inside one of these cave houses and got a surprise at the size. Where we ate was a room twelve by twelve, and eight foot high. The side of the walls had been smoothed with plaster and painted white, on the floor were home-made tiles with some design on them. It looked as if it had been mined, leaving enough wall for the outside, in which were cut doors and windows. These houses kept the same temperature all the year round. With the meal finished, the farmer brought out figs and nuts, then settled down for a long talk. No doubt he had never had this chance to find out so much about the outside world.

We talked well into the night and the conversation covered many subjects, from politics to what work the women did in our different countries. Many questions that were asked took me by surprise. I did not think these people would know so much, as many of them never leave the valley and hills in which they were born. With Gunner translating, I was able to follow most of the conversation and, with him throwing in a joke every now and then, he kept the whole family laughing. A friend of the family arrived up at the house to join the discussion. His wife was still quite pretty and showed little sign of the sixteen children that she had borne. When Gunner jokingly asked her husband how it was that Gunner himself was married and only had two children while he had sixteen, without batting an eyelid the farmer answered, "That's because my wife is here, and yours is in Norway." The laughter from everybody almost brought the roof down.

The women, including the blind one who sat spinning her wool all the time, asked as many questions as the men. The doorway was crowded with wide-eyed children who stood without a sound, but never missed a word that was said. On a wall hung one of their proudest possessions, a big, square diploma for dressmaking belonging to one of the daughters. Although a few of the farmers had sewing machines, none of them knew how to use them. When it was time to go to bed, the farmer insisted that we sleep there instead of along the road.

As we said goodnight, the two men asked us not to mention their names or what they had said regarding the political leader of their country, Franco. The farmer took up the kerosene light and asked us to follow, showing us first into a big bedroom about twenty-foot square and twelve-foot high. It was very clean and the double bed was covered with well-made, home-spun blankets. I hoped that he was going to kip me in with one of his daughters, but he led us out and up a steep track to a cave. In the dim light I could make out animals stabled inside, and the smell of urine was so strong that it would have brought tears to a glass eye. After collecting some bags there, he led us up a narrow track to a large cave house close to the top of a hill. It was empty and we soon had our beds made and turned in for the night.

In the morning, after a good sleep, we had a look around this place. It was very big and its emptiness magnified every sound we made. In one of the rooms was a four-furrow plough cut out of the limb of a tree and the points tipped with iron. There were four rooms as big as the bedroom we saw last night. The kitchen was smaller, and cut into the rock were a sink, a stove and an oven. In this place also, all the walls were plastered and the floor tiled. From the outside, all that could be seen of this big place was the front wall, in which holes for the door and window had been left. When it was being mined out, all of the work was done with a pick and shovel. The rock taken out was stacked against the hillside to form high walls and, when thick enough, a terrace is formed and rich soil placed on top and crops grown.

We made our way down to the farm where we were the night before. We had breakfast while the blind woman showed us how she made her cheese. Her kitchen was much the same, except the oven for making bread was much bigger. The roof was black from the smoke of many fires and the place was thick with flies, although she said there were not many but they were bad in the summer. She gave me some thick, lumpy, skimmed milk to try and I found it quite good. When we had finished breakfast we were asked not to go until her husband came back from work. He started at four o'clock every morning and came back around this time to milk and feed the animals, as the women were not allowed to touch them at all. When I told her that where I came from the women milked and worked in the tobacco, she asked me a good question, "How can they do all this and look after the house and the children?"

When the farmer arrived he was in a happy mood and glad that we had waited, as he wanted to show us his animals. The cave was much bigger than it looked in the dim light at night. At one end was their milking cow and her calf. The cow was also used for ploughing and on the wall close by was the yoke, carved by hand out of a tree, also the pigskin traces and plaited rope. At the other end were three goats used for milking. Baled hay was stowed up in the middle, and at the entrance was a pigsty in which one big, fat sow lay sleeping. We waited until the farmer had finished milking before we left, and he told us he was well off with his farm and stock. Many people owned no land at all and lived in just bare caves, working out on the farms for wages that they could hardly live on, as little as five shillings a day.

We took some photos, said goodbye and headed off along the road. The whole family watched and waved until we were out of sight. We walked along until we were looking down into the biggest valley, its deep path twisting and turning towards the sea. Hundreds of cave houses and caves dotted the walls of the valley, and row upon row of stone terraces reached from the floor of the valley like giant steps right to the top. On one side of the valley were the faint signs of former terraces, almost obliterated by time, the caves either buried or filled with silt. A lot of these terraces have been rebuilt, with the caves dug out and lived in just like their ancestors long years ago.

Who were the first builders of these caves? I do not know. The farmer knew only back to the Berbers, but before them I had heard of the people with blond hair and blue eyes, the last of them living high in the mountains in the steep and dangerous slopes. The caves are still there but to reach them time and equipment is needed, and as I tore my eyes away from the lofty peaks and started down the narrow, twisting track into the valley, I hoped that there would be another time. All the way down, people were working on their small blocks of land and crops, backs bent, swinging their broad-bladed, heavy hoes. The crops of potatoes, onions, tomatoes, maize, wheat, barley and corn were growing lush and virile in the rich, sweet-smelling earth.

Further down, on some of the wider places, were the big-stone circles used for threshing the grain. Close by some of these were the remains of old stone silos, the stone worn with age and filled with silt and rubble. Passing along the tracks were the little donkeys, their riders looking much too big for them. Some carried enormous loads of saltbush, so big that they could hardly move along the narrow track, while their owners, with a load half as big, walked behind holding onto their tails.

Almost at the bottom we met three women talking on the track. They greeted us, offered us some nuts to eat and talked with Gunner for a while. They had been planting, using wooden diggers cut from the branch of a tree. At the bottom we saw the first water, just a little pool filled by seepage. Although we saw seepage water in a few places later on, there was no sign of any streams or tanks. The valley appeared even more impressive looking up and along it from the bottom. It would have taken days to see it properly, wandering along the bed and gullies, over the many twisted tracks. We did not go into any of the caves on our way up. People greeted us all the way as they worked, drying-out their corn in the sun and making flour. Wide-eyed children watched as we passed, unmindful of the steep drop into the valley below, some of them showing the old bloodline with fair hair and pale skin.

The walk up to the top was pretty tough. Cactus grew, or had been planted, in clumps along the way. Although I kept a good lookout for any minerals in the rock formation, the only thing that I found was a small patch of black mica. Close to the top we stopped for a while and watched a farmer ploughing up a piece of land; his cow moving slowly, pulling the long-armed, wooden plough through the yielding soil. From the top of the ridge we looked out over more flat land, rich in colour; red, brown, yellow-looking, and black, that stretched across to the far distant coastline and joined the light blue of the sea. Tramping along the road once more, we passed a big plantation of young pines that would bring much-needed timber in years to come. Ahead of us the ground fell away into a deep crater, pitted and marked with different coloured bands of rock.

Even while we watched this long-dead crater that looked as if it could rumble and send up flame and lava at any moment, a heavy mist rolled in over the hills. It blanketed the mountains and seeped slowly into the crater, whirling around and down, giving an eerie appearance until it was covered and blotted out. As we moved on, the land became bare and cindery for miles with little to see. Following the winding road down into a dry, barren valley I saw the mullock heap of a mine, and I quickened my steps wondering what mineral they were digging for.

It was only a small place, with one building as a winch house and workshop, covering also the mouth of the shaft. There were six miners there and they showed us around the place. When I told them I had done a little bit of mining they asked if I would like to go down below and, although they had knocked off, they readily started all the machinery again, just so I could have a look around.

The shaft was circular, and twelve feet in diameter. When the carbide lamps were lit, three of us got into the bucket and the winch-man let us down slowly. Twenty feet down the collar set ended, all made of brick and cemented into place. The rough walls of the shaft closed in thirty feet below this to a width of eight feet. As we moved down the shaft it became cooler and finally the bucket came gently to rest near the bottom at one-hundred-and-forty feet. Looking up, the small circle of daylight looked far away, and below us was the well of the shaft. The water in there was used for boring out and was pumped through pipes along the drives by a portable, electric pump at the bottom.

The drive, or tunnel, was six feet high and four feet wide, and lit along the way by electric light. There were two tunnels each of which was a quarter-of-a-mile each. Where soft rock and faults had been found when driving, the walls and patches had been bricked up. There were no lines or trucks used to move all the rock and earth taken out. It all had to be wheeled out in a barrow along these long drives to the shaft, put into a bucket and at the top put back into a barrow and pushed to the mullock heap. There were a lot of questions I would have liked to ask, but because of the language difficulties I could not. I understood just enough to get by and was very surprised when they told me they were mining for water.

As we walked along, the miners pointed out all the small seepage places they had struck; the water from these flowing along drains in the tunnels to the shaft well. At the end of one of the tunnels was their electric boring plant set up at the face. It was a wonderful machine and the first of its type that I had seen. It had three speeds and used diamond bits, and they ran it for a while to show me how it worked. I gathered that their hope was to tap an underground stream, and the drill was twenty-four feet ahead. The other tunnel was driven at right angles to the one I was in, and work had stopped on it.

Back on top in the winch house I was able to find out what I wanted to know with the help of Gunner, and we sat and talked for a long time. They asked us many questions and told us of the poor wages they were paid. If they hit water they got a bonus. If they did not they got nothing. All expenses had to be paid out of their small wage and, after they had fired, they had to wait two days before going back down in the mine to clean out. They looked very unhappy after they asked me the wages in the mines in Australia, and I told them I had earned as much in two weeks as they got in six months. When we left we were given some figs and nuts and offered a lift to Las Palmas, but we wanted to have a look at the farms further on and made our way across the cinders to the road.

It was still a six-mile walk to the town of Valleseco, when we started to get the first of the rain that had been working up for most of the day. There was very little to see as the whole area was covered in low-lying cloud. When we finally turned into the more flat country, leaving the hills and caves behind, from deep down in the mist-covered valleys came the sound of the hoes striking on stone as the people worked. Further along, the laughter of the women and children drifted up to us as they gathered the chestnuts from the trees which had been planted along the slopes for miles. We passed farms all along the way; many of them having trees loaded with figs, lemons and oranges – as well as their usual crop of vegetables. Their boundaries were marked with six-foot high, stone walls which must have been a back-breaking job to build on some of the steeper slopes.

At the foot of a steep hill were bales of saltbush cut for fodder. We stopped for a while to watch a tiny figure make its way down the narrow track from the top, over steep-sided faces with a sheer drop to the bottom should he slip, with the heavy bale balanced on his shoulders. When he reached the road, he rose up and threw the bale down with the rest and dropped down exhausted. He was not very big and when he got his breath back enough to talk, we asked him the weight. I could not believe it when he told me two-hundred-and-fifty pounds. Gunner and I lifted it up, and found it was heavy for the two of us. We were told they do three to five trips a day to the top, cut the bush (sometimes going down the other side to get enough), then bale it and bring it down, using a sack folded corner-ways that fits over the forehead taking a little of the weight and ropes over the bale with cowhorn grips. For this they get paid a few pence a pound. While we were there, the truck came from town to pick up the load and we watched the weighing for a bit. Most of the bales were over two hundred pounds, and those that were under belonged to the young boys around sixteen or seventeen years old who were just starting the game.

The weighing was crudely done by the driver, a big bloke who looked as if he did not like work. The scales hung in the centre of a long pole and the bale was lifted off the ground by a hook on the scale. The men worked hard on one end of the pole standing on tip toes, stretching their trembling arms high above their head, straining to lift the bale clear of the ground. The driver, grinning all the time, was lowering his end so that a good part of the weight was lost with the bale resting on the ground. After watching this driver rob these poor, hard-working people out of their money whilst grinning at them, I moved off down the road before I gave way to an urge to put my boot in him where it would hurt the most.

It was dark when we got to Valleseco and we had a good meal at a small café: soup, steak, fruit and white wine. I think the steak was a piece of horse or donkey, but it tasted good just the same. We had hoped to spend a few more days in the hills but, as the rain had set in, we decided to return to our boats and caught a bus back.

In the morning, I saw that the boys had not been idle while I was away. Bill had painted all the seams along the side white to stop them from opening up in the hot weather, and the boat looked like a barber's pole with the white stripes on the grey. We left it like this for over a week before painting the side white because of the oil on the water, and I don't think that one boat passed by without asking why we painted stripes on it. Of course we told them that we just wanted to be different. They rowed away and left us alone, but called us such names as 'Striped Dragon', 'White Dragon', 'White-Striped Grey Dragon', and behind our backs I am sure the 'mad Australians'.

While we were waiting for our sails, some of the small boats began the long trip across the Atlantic. The two big schooners left a few days after our arrival. Next to leave was a thirty-two-foot gaff ketch, built by a young American in England. The two young Jewish men started early one morning in their twenty-two-foot sloop. 'The Black Swan', Tyrone Power's yacht and the 'Lenney' sailed together, both under the English flag. The 'Aku' sailed a couple of days later, continuing her round-the-world voyage after a year in harbour. The home-built plywood boat 'Four Square' followed with two men on board, hoping for a fast passage.

At long last our sails were ready and the sailmaker brought them down. What a good set of sails they were; strong and all hand-stitched, the stitching neat and showing the good workmanship. The cost was less than half of what it would have been in England. The next day Duff and I went to the market to get our fresh stores: one-hundred pounds of potatoes, fifty pounds of onions, twenty-five pounds of tomatoes at two pence a pound, tinned milk, dried fruit and many other odds and ends. We took the boat alongside the wall and filled our water tank, and while I tried to clean some of the oil off the dinghy, Bill went around to one of the British destroyers in port to see if he could get some books to read. He came back bent double with half-a-mail-sack full over his shoulder.

Back in harbour, Gunner said he would follow us in two days, and our other friend, a Rhodesian, would leave as soon as he put his mast back in after shortening it six feet. A tough man, this bloke, having his second try at the crossing. His first boat hit a log of timber in a gale off the French coast, and for three days and nights he battled to keep it afloat until it was dismasted and he was taken off by the Yarmouth lifeboat just before it sank. Another boat ready to leave was the thirty footer built for Lindeman, the canoeist, sailed by a sixty-five-year-old American who was more at home swinging from a bosun-chair up the mast than a rocking chair. Six British yachts, two French and one German were all getting ready to leave. Nearly all of them were around thirty feet in length. If you could see the positions of all of the boats on a chart, there would be a long line of these small boats stretching from the Canaries to the West Indies.

The thirty-foot steel boat 'Frisk' sailed in the afternoon, and at eight o'clock in the morning we pulled up the anchor, motored across to Gunner's boat to say goodbye, and then passed close to the destroyer, yelling out our thanks as we went. Then we were around the corner and the swells started to roll in as we braced our legs against the heaving deck and bent on the sails.

Chapter Seven

Canary Islands to West Indies

We sailed along under the fore-and-aft rig all morning, and then put up our spinnakers for the first time. There was no trouble. Nothing went wrong. Bill tied the sheets to the tiller and from then on the boat sailed itself, keeping a good, steady course. We ran parallel with the island for the rest of the day with little to do except watch the changing colours of the fields and mountains as the sun grew lower in the sky. It was the first time that the three of us were able to sit down in the cabin together and have tea and a talk while the boat rolled on her way with the wind dead aft. The three of us felt the motion a bit after being so long in harbour and none of us got much sleep the first couple of nights.

It was hard to go to sleep knowing that no-one was at the helm to keep a lookout for ships and we all kept waking up hearing sounds and going on deck for a look around. It was just as well, for one night Bill got up and looked out the forward hatch to see the lights of a boat coming in our direction and had to use the torch on the sails. This is the only fault I can find with self-steering and it took me over a week to get used to it before I was able to get a good night's sleep. The wind blew strongly for a couple of days and then started to ease off slowly, although it did not always blow us on exactly the course we wanted. We were contented to let the wind take us around in a slow curve while we spent most of our time trying to catch fish. Duff caught the first fish on the fifth day out; a three-foot barracuda, and before it had time to gasp its last breath it was in the pan for breakfast. From then on everyone had fish fever.

The wind dropped right away until we were just being wafted along with a two-knot breeze. The sea was calm and sometimes like a mirror, so that the sun shining through the sails reflected deep down in the clear, blue water like a star sapphire. We spent a lot of time swimming over the side in the warm water or laying on deck in the sun reading, but never a day went past without some bit of excitement. As soon as Duff had caught the fish we rigged the harpoon up for sharks and bigger fish. After tea that night as we all sat on deck and watched the sunset while Duff strummed a tune on the guitar, a sunfish circled the boat. It was huge, almost circular in side view, and would have been between two-hundred-and-fifty to three hundred pounds in weight. It swam around with a strange, yawing motion, its long dorsal fin breaking the water like a shark.

It seemed very interested in the boat and swam around and around it, not a bit worried about the commotion it had caused as the three of us tried to get harpoon, wire and rope up from the cockpit to the bowsprit across the dinghy, under booms and around the sails. When it was all ready and I was about to throw, the sunfish gave a flick with its anal fins and disappeared. To make sure I would not get caught the same way again, I spliced together some of Bill's halyards and made a good, strong line with six feet of wire on the harpoon end and an eye splice at the other so some more rope could be bent on if needed. Just before the end we put on a big, plastic float we had found in the sea in case we hit something too big.

During these calms and light winds, fish were all around us; tunny jumping out of the water on all sides swimming ahead of us and under the boat. When this happened Duff would have Bill in the water like a well-trained pointer, face mask on, hanging on to the bobstay with one hand, pointing out the shoal of fish with the other, while he threw his line among them time and time again. Once in a while, one of the fish would follow the lure up, but most times they would ignore it, and after days of trying he finally caught one only to lose it when his line broke.

Many times Bill went in with his face mask and spear gun only to have the spear miss by inches as the gun was very poor, a cheap one bought in Spain that shot no more than two feet high. I missed many a fish with the harpoon as they followed a lure to the surface and it was just bad luck that we were not eating fish every day. I think a rod would be handy for tuna and if you carried a little gelignite on board, well, you could not miss! If we had carried a crossbow or at least a bow and arrow we would have filled our cockpit with fish.

One particular day when there was no wind, the sea dead flat and the early afternoon sun beating down on the boat, making the decks too hot to stand on, the three of us were listless and tired as we lay around waiting for some wind. Duff was on deck lying in the shade of a small sail when he saw a fin cutting the water not far from the boat. His yell brought us all on deck, and after one look the chase was on. Like a well-practised manoeuvre, we went into action. Sails were dropped in seconds, Duff was down below busy turning on water cocks and priming the motor, Bill was unlashing the tiller and getting ready to crank, while up forward I got the harpoon and line ready. The motor started easily and we were away after the fast, disappearing fish.

For half an hour the chase was on as the fish cut through the clear water, twisting and turning, zigzagging ahead of us. As we got closer we saw it was a six-foot swordfish swimming strongly ahead of the boat with a zigzag motion, sometimes making sharp turns so that we had to make a big circle before we could catch up again. Duff, high on the dinghy, kept him in sight all the time shouting directions to Bill, jumping up and down like a Maori doing the haka, while Bill, down in the cockpit, could see nothing and had an expression on his face, like the captain of a destroyer going through an enemy minefield. Up at the bowsprit I waited, knowing that if I missed I could expect a good ear-bashing and dark scowls for breakfast instead of fish. My first throw fell much too short, the second missed by inches, and I waited until the fish was about fifteen feet ahead of the bowsprit before I threw for the third time. The harpoon flew straight and true and hit the swordfish two feet ahead of the tail, held for a moment, then came out as he shot forward with terrific speed and disappeared for good. The harpoon head did not penetrate far enough before it opened as it was the pivot type, so I put a stronger lashing on it for next time. Although we did not get any fish it certainly livened the day up a bit.

We had three days of dead calm when the boat hardly moved at all. Even though we were not getting anywhere, I liked these days the best as it gave us a good chance to see the marine life we would have missed if the water had been more boisterous. Many strange creatures floated past the boat during these calms and we spent a lot of time in the water or hanging over the side with the face mask on watching them pass by. We started off with having one tiny, striped, pilot fish swimming around the keel and ended up with a dozen riding the wave in front of the bow, fanning out ahead like scouts, darting to and fro to inspect any small object that drifted past. Portuguese men-of-war floated quietly past with their pink-tinged oval sails above the water using the wind for steering as well as to propel them on their way. Sometimes the water was cloudy with zoo plankton, so small that they could not be seen with the naked eye, and quite large, feathery and plant-like forms moved past about two fathoms down. Many types of jelly-like animals swam slowly past, all different shapes and sizes, and we caught several of these using a cloth water-strainer on a mop handle for a scoop and the pressure cooker became an observation tank. Some of these jelly-type creatures had small, brown shrimps inside them, still alive, that crawled out on our open palm. Most of these creatures had some form of lumination at night, and the water was filled with purple dots and glows and sometimes bright flashes as big as dinner plates.

Although there was a fair bit of phosphorescence in the water at night around the boat, there was nowhere the amount that we sailed through off Spain. The water there was just a glowing mass. Just before dawn I noticed that many of these creatures headed back down to the lower levels

Crossing Atlantic under spinnakers.

for the day-time, coming to the surface only at night. If I ever did another trip like this I would carry a bit of equipment such as a fine, mesh net and a small trawl, and perhaps a microscope. Many interesting hours could be spent in these calm waters when there is no wind. Two pods of small whales passed by; one heading north, the other south. They swam around us for quite a while but would come no closer than fifteen feet off the boat. The largest of these whales would have been thirty feet long.

The first and only shark we had seen so far came up astern of us while we were busy seeing who could dive the deepest to a mark on the leadline. We sighted him a few hundred yards away, and before the word "shark" was out properly, the three of us were back on board dripping water and getting the harpoon and ropes ready. However, the shark moved away, cruised past us at five hundred yards and all our yelling and splashing in the water would bring him no closer. It was just as well as he was much too big for the harpoon. We filled in a bit of time in these calms doing a few odd jobs on the boat and some painting on deck.

We put the dinghy over the side so I could row ahead and take some photos of the boat under spinnakers. It turned out quite a job as the sun had opened the seams of the dinghy and it leaked like a sieve. It was a race against time and the water, with me trying to use two cameras, balance myself in the tossing dinghy and keep the boat in the viewfinder as it rolled something terrible. By the time the boat caught up with me the dinghy was full of water and the cameras held high above my head.

A wind came up after these calms and pushed us along steadily for three days. The only thing that happened during this time was the canary, who proved to be a very good sailor and had given us no trouble, got out of his cage while Duff was cleaning it, took a magnificent lunge from the deck towards the heavens, flapped his wings about three times and then did a nose dive into the sea. Once again sails were dropped and the dinghy thrown over the side. However one oar was being used for a boom for the second mizzen so I jumped into the dinghy and using one oar, paddled after the small yellow speck on the blue sea. By the time Bill and Duff had the motor started I had caught up with the bird and when they came alongside I was sitting in the dinghy, looking very forlorn with the water lapping around my thighs, holding a small, wet bundle gently in my hand. It looked very dead except for the water coming out of its beak. We put it in the cage and it laid without moving for about an hour, just a bundle of wet, yellow feathers, then he stood up, shook himself and jumped on the perch. He then seemed to have a relapse because he did not move all day, but next morning he was O.K. and ate like a pig, throwing water from his bath over anyone that came within three feet of his cage and puffing his chest out as if to say, "Well, there are not many canaries who have been for a swim in the Atlantic".

It was next morning at eight o'clock on the twenty third of November, fourteen days from Las Palmas, that we sighted the Cape Verde Islands, forty miles off the port bow. All day the wind was light, but that night it came up strong and we had the north-east trades at last. With the trades behind us the miles surged past our bow, the spinnakers ballooned out ahead like two giant wings and two small mizzens set aft added their little bit to our average of over a hundred miles a day. Duff's fishing lines astern were starting to bring in the fish. First a nice tuna, then three big bonitos. Quite a few times his lines have been smashed up by very big fish and once he pulled the line in to find the hook imbedded in the jaw bone of what would have been a big barracuda. I think many fish are lost this way as our speed through the water would tear the hook out.

With the wind still holding strong we passed the half-way mark, the boat doing around a hundred-and-twenty-five miles a day. For the last week the seas have been very confused, coming in on our quarters, stern and beam making it extremely uncomfortable and we are all feeling the lack of sleep. The only trouble we have had so far was when one of the tiller lines parted throwing one of the spinnaker booms forward and sheering off the pin holding the boom on the mast band. Luckily there were two pins and after rigging it again we were on our way.

The days passed swiftly marked only by the sunsets, each one seemingly better than the day before. The weeks were marked by Sunday when we all had a shave, and at midday the most important thing happened, what we had waited and counted the days for: we opened a tin of peaches and cream. In no time they disappeared and the plates licked clean with much gusto. The only sound to be heard was the smacking of lips and then "roll on next Sunday". The supply of fresh vegetables was dwindling rapidly and the freshwater tank gave an ominous ring when tapped. Although there were rain showers around the horizon, so far not one drop had fallen on our deck.

There was still plenty to do on board. Both Duff and I were learning navigation and even I, with my big, splay fingers, managed to get a bit of a strum out of the guitar, but only just. Most of the books have been thrashed pretty well, and I am sure that Duff knows some chapters of "Lady Chatterley's Lover" off by heart. We have started to read a few chapters of the Bible every night, it passes the time well and finishes a lot of arguments that we have had in the past, as well as starting a lot of new ones. We had to remind ourselves that it had been altered many times in translation, and not always for the right reasons. Most people in those days could not read or write and when we compared the accounts of some eyewitnesses we were led to believe some of them could have done with glasses. We started to put a light up in the rigging as even way out here a ship cut our course a few nights ago, less than a mile away.

On the first of December the winds started to fall away and were light for five days before they picked up again. It was on the fifth day, when the seas were calm, we saw another shark cruising astern of us. He stopped about thirty feet away for a long while and took no notice of Bill kicking his feet in the water or the red plastic bucket that Duff threw in front of him to bring him closer. Even a bit of blood that I managed to squeeze out of a cut on my wrist did not bring him any nearer. Finally, in his own good time, with one of our pilot fish in the lead, he nosed up to the boat to have a look around and got the harpoon in his belly. As soon as the harpoon struck he swerved sharply then cruised slowly around. The six-foot harpoon sticking out of him bothered him as much as if it were a match stick. He was seven-feet long and light in colour. We had him on the line for about a minute before the harpoon pulled out, the barb failing to open, and away went our shark steak dinner. The shank of the harpoon was bent like a bow, even though it was half-inch steel. At no time did this shark cruise with its dorsal fin above the water and we would not have seen it if there was any sea running. So now our swims are limited to a very fast plunge over the side, just in and out, or a bucket bath on the bobstay.

On Saturday, the ninth of December, we celebrated our month at sea in grand style by opening a tin of plum pudding; one of the two that we had on board in case we had to spend Christmas Day at sea, and by adding a tin of fruit to it plus a custard that Bill made, we had a champion meal. That gave Bill and Duff something to talk about besides the long-digested meals eaten in the past that they persist in re-eating again. So vivid are their descriptions of fried chicken, underdone steak, baked potatoes, fresh green peas and lobster salad, that I can stand it no longer and have to go down below, where I cannot hear them. Judging by the rapt expressions on their faces you would think they had just finished such a meal and were busy wiping the grease off their fingers on the tablecloth when no-one is looking.

The noon sight today put us on Latitude 13° 38 minutes north and we have to run down to 13° 10 minutes to be on the latitude of Barbados and still have a distance of five hundred miles to go. The winds have remained constant these last few days and although we have travelled a lot of miles there has been no sign of any fish for over a week. Even the flying fish seem to have deserted us. Almost every morning we have been able to go on deck and pick them up, from the size of a small butterfly to a foot long, but not now. Even the shoals that would suddenly appear out of the water in front of the bow and glide for an amazing distance over and between the waves, the sun glittering on their outstretched wings, no longer appear to break the monotony of the sea.

The motion of the boat has been much better since the wind came up again, the seas more even and longer, like the ones we expected in the trades and we had heard so much about. We used the last of our potatoes and onions on the tenth. We put all of these into a big stew that would have lasted us three days, but after the first meal of it all our constipation was cured immediately and when we got around to inspecting it next morning, the top of it was covered in foam and had a sour smell, probably owing to a bad tin of something that was put into it. We gave it the deep six and settled back to cold meals, as our kerosene ran out the same day, having lost some through a leaking can.

The water in our main tank lasted well and we drank the last of it next day. It was pretty thick by then and tasted brackish but the water in our last two-gallon can was as good as the day we filled it. We have all lost a bit of weight. Duff does not show it much but Bill is only a shadow of his old self, and as for me if my ribs are not showing I know I am starting to live too well. It surprised me how out of condition we were. Just a little thing like climbing up the mast made me sit down as if I had just finished four hours' work.

We had expected to sight the island of Barbados on the thirteenth in the late afternoon, but sighted its low outline about thirty-five miles away at seven o'clock in the morning, the current putting us a little more ahead than we allowed for. Having made sure that it was the island and not a cloud we were in jubilant spirits for a while, but knowing how long it would take us to get there we all turned in and slept for a couple of hours. After breakfast we took our spinnakers down and hoisted the fore-and-aft rig, but later dropped our headsails, put a spinnaker up and moved along before a nice breeze.

After dinner the island began to take shape; the low, rolling land with blurred patches of green and darker spots formed fields and houses, the sun reflecting off windows and roof tops. We passed many small fishing-boats on our way in bobbing about like corks and remarked, "Look at them mad bastards," but no doubt they were saying something equally as pleasant about us, though I would not like to have changed places with any of them. Drawing closer to the island it was a pleasure to sit and look at the freshness of the fields, tinted here and there with patches of red flowers, the trees with their trunks and limbs bent to the direction and might of the trade winds. The only sound out here was the water against the bow making no more noise than a small creek after it has come from the mountains and reached the flat land below.

Unfortunately, as it must, the sounds of civilisation came to us as we drew nearer, the scream of a jet plane taking off from some airport, the honking and blowing of horns from buses and cars, but the noise did not spoil it too much as we sailed along the island. All the buildings were spread out as they should be and not crowded and dirty like many of the places we visited. Plenty of beautiful, white beaches here with a background of tall palms and West Indians swimming and laughing in the warm sunshine. With all the land noises coming to us, the sea reminded us that it was not to be forgotten. In the background was the sound of rollers breaking on the reefs just in case we might forget.

When we went around the black buoy into Carlisle Bay we knew that our long trip was almost over, because our course from Las Palmas was in a big curve. We logged over three thousand one hundred miles for thirty-four days, and when we tried to start the motor to take her in we found that the petrol had evaporated in the tank and so took her in under sail. Behind us the sun was setting and when we dropped the anchor at last we only had time to turn around and look at the bright red horizon, the sun already below it, and watch the night come down like a giant curtain slowly closing over the red.

Chapter Eight

Barbados and St Lucia

The launch with the port doctor and Customs Officer was alongside as soon as the anchor was down and the formalities quickly finished with. All we had to do was get dressed, wait for the boat that the Customs men promised to send straight back and we would be able to get the feel of dry land again. After an hour had passed and the boat had not arrived, we knew we would not be going ashore that night as we were anchored too far out and our dinghy was leaking so badly that we would not have been able to go a third of the distance without swamping. The only thing left was to accept the invitation that was shouted to us as we passed the big yacht 'DoDo To', "come and have a cold beer off the ice".

Although the yacht was only a few hundred yards away, Bill and I were hard pressed to get there before the dinghy sank. We made it with the boat half full and Bill bailing like a madman, and after emptying it out I started back for Duff. Half-way I had to stop rowing and bail. In the end, with the dinghy awash and oars floating away, the swell picked the dinghy up, overturned it, and I had two oars, a cushion and a plastic bucket to hold on to while I tried to turn the dinghy back up. Finally I managed and wedged one of the oars under the seat with the bucket, tied the cushion to the painter and kneeling down with the water up to my neck, started to paddle back, mentally working out how far I could jam the oar down the mouth of a shark I was sure would show up at any moment. It seemed like an hour before I was alongside shouting abuse at Duff who was trying hard not to laugh, and with some more dry clothes on and a

St. Lucia, West Indies.

new pair of rowlocks, we started off again with Duff bailing fifty to the dozen and me rowing as if I was in a sculling championship.

We wondered if the beer would be worth it, but it was. The first one tasted marvellous, the second one even better, and after the third one the skipper informed us he liked his drop of beer and said as soon as we finish a bottle to throw it over the side and we would have a full one in our hand before it hit the water. As we had bent the elbow a bit in our time and were partial to the odd glass, the sound of the bottles hitting the water came fairly regularly as the night wore on.

I don't know what time I departed from the land of the living, but I woke up to find myself still on the yacht and the skipper standing over me with an evil grin on his face, handing me a fresh bottle of beer to start the day off right. In no time at all Duff and I were matching the skipper drink for drink. Bill was feeling a little worse for wear so he just sat back and took it easy. The skipper's wife cooked a big pile of pancakes for breakfast, enough for about six men, but the three of us managed to put them away in record time.

It was not until one o'clock in the afternoon that we finished drinking by mutual consent and we made our way back to our boat, leaving the skipper with an empty ice box and sitting somewhat glassy eyed in the saloon talking to himself. Of course Duff and I had to do something brilliant like swim back to the boat instead of going in the dinghy. I just managed to make it back after swallowing many mouthfuls of salt water and hung there without the energy to haul myself on board. The motor boat from the big yacht, with motor roaring, went after Duff who was swimming out to sea in the general direction of Australia. He, too, swallowed a fair bit of salt water and looked more dead than alive when he finally landed back on board. I don't think any one of us will forget our greeting after the crossing. I know I will not forget the granddaddy of all hangovers that I had for the next three days.

There was not much we could do in Barbados except walk around with empty pockets. Our enquiries for work brought nothing. A reporter from the town paper came on board for a story and gave us a good write-up under the heading "Looking for Work", but it brought no results. We decided to split our money up, nine pounds for stores left each of us with eight pounds. A few of mine went to send cards and notes to New Zealand, and a couple of outings to the pictures made my bank-roll look pretty sick. Bill and I would pound the pavement into town every day and buy our food. It was hard to pass by the cafes, smell the steak cooking, look at all the fruit at the market and not be able to buy any. I cannot say that we were hungry, but then we were never full either. Always we had that hollow feeling.

Duff invested his money in the usual way. He disappeared one day around twelve with that look in his eyes and had not returned by the time Bill and I went ashore at sundown. It was while we were sitting quietly on the quay watching a West Indian schooner come in that he bumped into us. Our peace was shattered by a terrible yell that made heads turn a block away and Duff came into view, pushing through the crowd, dragging a girl behind him as if she were a sack of potatoes. He was quite drunk and had already reached the sentimental stage and started to proclaim us for long-lost mates, five hundred yards away, as if he had not seen us for a year. At five yards, he swung the girl around and presented her to us as though she were Marilyn Monroe. I must admit she was a bit of an eye opener, though I would have rather kept mine shut and denied knowing him at all. I tried to keep a straight face while I sized up the girl. She was dressed in a red blouse and a striped skirt, with a sailor's hat on her head on which was written, in big red letters "Eat at Joe's Diner" and the address.

It took us half an hour before we were able to get rid of Duff without hurting his feelings. My parting advice to him was, "Remember son, you cannot go to sea with VD", but it fell on deaf ears and the last time we saw him he was weaving his way up the street, holding tightly to the girl in case somehow she managed to get away, unmindful of the spectators and the stares he was getting. It was twelve o'clock the next day before we saw him again, portraying the perfect example of a beachcomber as he walked along the white sand with a background of tall palms. He was unheedful of the breakers washing over his bare feet, his unshaven chin sunk low on his chest, his eyes staring at the sand around his feet, his white pants so filthy that they would never be white again, his shirt flapping in the wind with all the buttons torn off in a fight and his bare chest matted with hair covered in sand. Back on board he said very little, which was strange. Then he turned in and slept for eight hours solid.

We stayed in Barbados five days. Some of our mail had gone adrift and was sent to British Guyana so only Bill got a couple of letters. It was a pity we were not able to have a look around this pretty island with all its fields and cane. Here it is called 'Little England' and from the sea you could very well be coming up on the Isle of Wight. I found the people very pleasant. It was their voices that I liked the most. Many of them spoke with a soft, liquid tone. 'Corney the Yank' arrived two days after us and had some hair-raising tales to tell of his trip across; sixteen days from the Cape Verde Islands and using his motor ten hours a day. He had more trouble than Flash Gordon, including the unpleasant task of pumping seventy gallons of fuel out of his bilge. One of his skin fittings fractured, water started to pour into the boat and as it took a while to find he was sure that his last day had come. Now he swears that if ever he gets his ship back, never will he set foot on the sea again, claiming that anyone who goes to sea is mad and that by the time we reach New Zealand we will all be ready for the nut house. I have to admit that he never was a sailor, and he never would be one. The 'Aku' arrived while we were there after a trip of twenty-eight days from the Verdes, thirty-nine days for the whole trip. He, too, had light winds.

We sailed from Barbados on the nineteenth of December and although we did not see much we had a good rest and enjoyed the warm sunshine and the clear water. The trip to St Lucia was a rough one, with heavy rain and squalls most of the night. Although we sighted the island at two o'clock in the morning it was not until one in the afternoon when we sailed into the harbour. We had to tack in and the wind squalls coming out of the gullies and valleys in the surrounding hills made the old boat heel over so much I thought that we would lose some gear. However, everything held and we dropped our sails a hundred yards from the wharf. I managed to make a big hit with the Customs Officer, who was yelling and waving, by almost skewering him with the bowsprit when I pulled alongside. For all that he was not too hard on us and went away satisfied with three crew lists in his hand. Some enterprising West Indian tried to sell us water at fifty cents a gallon, but got such a tongue lashing from the three of us that he showed us where the tap was, even helped carry the water back on board and did not take a cent.

I liked St Lucia right from the start, with its tropical vegetation coming right down to the palms on the foreshore and the buildings dotted on the slopes around the bay. The little bay with all the yachts in which had the appropriate name of 'Whiskey Hollow' we avoided, and anchored perhaps a little too close to the rubbish dump, but at least there we were left alone. The closest boat to us was an old West Indian sloop with its telegraph pole mast on which fluttered an old Australian flag. It was now used as a rubbish barge. Fifty yards off along an old wall the fishermen sat in their canoes with their broad brimmed straw hats on, rigging their lines for fishing. Behind them was the net in a long line drying in the sun. About a dozen children swam stark naked close by, laughing and playing. With Christmas coming on, I kept an eye on a big sow and her litter that were foraging not too far away in the rubbish.

We started the hunt for work the next day and I looked around for any sort of mining or drilling. While we were waiting we did the old boat up a bit, doing the top, sides and the varnish work again. Duff was the first to start work just two days before Christmas at a beach club doing a bit of cooking, barman and waiter. He took off to his new job leaving us on board with a few of the local prostitutes he managed to round up, three bunches of bananas and very little else. I managed to get a bit of pork at the market for Christmas dinner, and with a few odds and ends plus the tin of peaches and pudding still left on board, we would not fare too badly.

Christmas Day was also Bill's birthday and he did not even get a card. When we woke up in the morning we found that one of the yachts had left a bottle of whiskey and a tinned whole chicken in the cockpit. I don't think they will ever know just how much that meant to us. I know that no Christmas will ever go by without me remembering that one kind thought. Having planned to cook dinner in the evening, all our plans went astray when Bill got a trip down to the Grenadines on a sixty-foot schooner and sailed at three o'clock. I saw no use in opening a tin of chicken for myself, so got drunk, had a bit of bread and went to sleep.

Boxing Day I cooked up a good feed, rounded up a couple of girls from ashore to eat with me, then Duff arrived with another bottle of whiskey. We had a good session and the girls had a good meal. For the next five days, I led an idle life just laying on the deck in the sun and swimming. The three bunches of bananas ripened all together, so I had bananas for breakfast, dinner and tea. On the thirty-first, a thirty-footer arrived in the harbour bound for Australia and the next day, with all the money gone, I started work at the beach club with Duff.

I was a little worried about leaving the boat in the harbour with nobody on board, but the problem was solved when Bill arrived back an hour before I was due to start work. I sat for a while watching him work around on the deck of the schooner, polishing brass, wiping down the varnish work, but what really made me look was when the charters were ready to go ashore, how smartly he jumped into the dinghy and mopped the seats so they would not get their bottoms damp and my laughter and comments did not make him feel any better. When he finally came on board, I could see that he was madder than I had ever seen him in the three years I had known him.

It turned out that the captain, a good man in harbour, was a holy terror at sea. Bill had been on deck for thirty hours. None of the crew was allowed to go below and rest. The two West Indian crew were treated and spoken to like dogs so, like the rest they only lasted one trip and were waiting to go ashore and feel like human beings again. Bill refused to sail on the ship again at any price so I left him on board and headed for the beach club, wondering how he would get on when the girls from the rum shop arrived yelling out and looking for a meal.

Arriving at the beach club feeling decidedly ill at ease, I was even more so when I saw the place with its marble floor, the big, plush couches of different colours and paintings hung everywhere. As if they did not have enough colour in the place they handed me a bright red shirt to wear and so I started work at a job that I never thought I would do. The first night there were forty guests for dinner and Duff was in his element, moving among them with a speed only acquired through practice, serving a six-course dinner, never once getting ruffled and always polite. He had to put up with a lot that night and still smile. Had it been me I would have been fired, because I could not have resisted the temptation to spill a bowl over one or two of them.

They ran Duff's feet off him that night and quite a few tried to get me from behind the bar, but no amount of whistling or "hey boy!" moved me. I stood stone-faced behind the bar, polishing imaginary fly specks off the glasses. I did not even see the bloke who stood up on his chair and waved his hands as if he was the batman on an aircraft carrier bringing a plane into land. The only people I left the bar for to get their order were those who showed some manners. The rest walked up to the bar or caught Duff. I was not surprised to see the elite men of the town: the lawyers, the big shop owners, politicians, acting no differently than sailors on leave, and some of their girlfriends and daughters beat the rum-shop whores hands down when it came to soliciting.

Duff and I got to bed at four in the morning and then up again at six, all for the large sum of fifteen shillings a day and food, if we could find any. To tell the truth, I ate better on the boat. At least I felt full occasionally. Our bed consisted of sleeping on the couches in the bar and we were usually so tired we could have slept on a barbed-wire fence. I learnt and saw a lot during the little time I was there and did things I never thought I would, like keeping my mouth shut as I stood in front of a little Englishwoman while she bashed my ears for fifteen minutes because her bath water was five minutes late, and then, with her head reaching no higher than my chest, she would stick her two hands up level with my face and count off on her fingers all the things that were not just right yesterday.

I turned out to be a very poor barman. I was forever getting the drinks mixed up. With a tray loaded with rums, whiskeys, cokes, rum and coke, tonic, and gin and tonic, I usually had the most trouble and after setting the drinks out, I would beat it back to the bar before the coughs and splutters told me that I had got it wrong again.

There were always a few guests staying at the club and they gave us plenty of work to do, running between the bar and the bungalows with their drinks and anything else they needed. Mostly they were nice people, like an American couple who forgave me when on the first morning I gave them their fruit juice with a big cockroach breaststroking around the top of the glass. The brigadier, "retired India", and his wife were sticklers for routine and their days never varied from breakfast in the morning to their sundowner at night. If their tea was not there dead on four o'clock, it was a major crisis. It was me who committed the most unforgivable sin that made the brigadier yell as if he had just sat on a hat pin and sent people hurrying around as if one of the bungalows was on fire. However, Duff came straight to me and I had to admit feeling like a schoolboy who had just been caught stealing apples, because I was the one who gave the brigadier sour milk in his tea.

There were guests almost every night for dinner and most of these would ask for drinks that I had never heard of before: Bloody Mary, Green Goddess and all sorts of liqueurs that would send me out to Duff in the kitchen with my book and pencil to find out what the hell they were talking about and how to mix it. Only one person while I was there made a mistake and asked the boss if the whiskeys were getting smaller. From then on, I lined his glasses up along the bar and waited with the bottle until he looked around for his drinks. Then I looked him straight in the eyes and poured. He got the idea and there were no more complaints from him.

One of the strangest groups we had for dinner was from the local churches. I was busy with a barman's favourite occupation, mopping the bar, when the door opened and in walked three ministers with their collars back-to-front, followed by their wives dressed in black and their daughters bringing up the rear their eyes downcast, looking as if they were ashamed to be in such a place. They sat down quietly and folded their hands on their laps, and it looked to me as if they were going to start a prayer meeting as they talked together in hushed tones. I had no intention of going anywhere near them, but the boss told me to take their order, so away I went. I stood by their table for about a minute, waiting, but they took no more notice of me than they would a piece of furniture. In the end, looking more like a standover man than a waiter and speaking in rather a coarse voice, so Duff told me later, I asked in a loud voice, "What ya want to drink?" Their shocked silence and reactions would not have been any different had I shouted out that misused four-letter word right in their faces. The shocked silence continued for over a minute. No-one looked at me. Everyone seemed interested in their shoes all of a sudden. One or two tightened their hands on their laps and judging by the way some of the lips were moving I was sure some of them were praying against this temptation that had suddenly been flung in their midst. After another half a minute of ensuing silence, I came to the conclusion that they were not the drinking kind and made my way back to the bar. The boss had other ideas and sent me back to try again. After repeating the performance and waiting for another half a minute, a timid voice spoke up and asked for 'one Coke', and with a sigh of relief I went back to the bar. Still the boss was not satisfied, went to try his luck himself and managed to squeeze another Coke and a small wine out of the crowd.

With the announcement that dinner was ready, the group filed off as if they were going to a funeral, sat down and grace was said. It was then that the boss started to give me instructions on how I had to pour the wine. It seemed to me that it was a lot of trouble to go to over a bottle of wine and my suggestion that the bottle should be placed on the table and let them help themselves was met with a blank stare. The boss himself opened the bottle in case I should sample the wine before the host and away I went and poured just the right amount in the host's glass and stepped back, waiting for him to try it. It was then that we reached a deadlock. For a minute or more I stood, waiting for him to try the wine, while he sat looking at me, probably wondering what the hell I was standing there for, and in the end I just started to pour around the table, but what looked like a simple job turned out an endurance test as hands were put over glasses just in the act of pouring and fingers were cocked, raised or lowered according to the amount wanted. One old lady kept me in suspense while I poured a thimbleful of wine in her glass, drop by drop, so by the time I had finished the table my hand was shaking so much I could hardly hit the glass. After that night I decided that it was just not the job for me and longed to be back on the boat at sea again.

Chapter Nine

Cruising the West Indies

It was not long after this that I got my chance to get away from the beach club for a while when two American women chartered the boat to take them to Martinique, a French island thirty-six miles away. After warning them about the size of the boat and what they could expect, they still wanted to go instead of flying as they knew we needed the money and they wanted to see what it was like to sail. We were a little late leaving as Bill had trouble getting the ice they had asked for so they could drink rum on the way across, though I doubted if there would be much drunk once we got out a bit.

It turned out one of those days that you dream about and very seldom get. The wind was right behind us coming out of the harbour, outside the sea was calm with a good wind on the beam that took us all the way to Martinique. It was a beautiful, clear day with the long outline of the island against the blue sea. Even before we were half-way we could pick our landmark, Diamond Rock, against the island. By dinner time it was obvious that it was going to take a lot longer to reach the island than we had first thought. The older of the two women was feeling sea-sick, and judging by her groan as she laid on the deck and watched their plane fly overhead, I think she would have given a lot to have been on it. The other one enjoyed it all the way and never stopped drinking rum. Of course I did my best to keep up with her but I think she was a few ahead of me by the time we anchored.

We made good time between the islands but off Diamond Rock, in

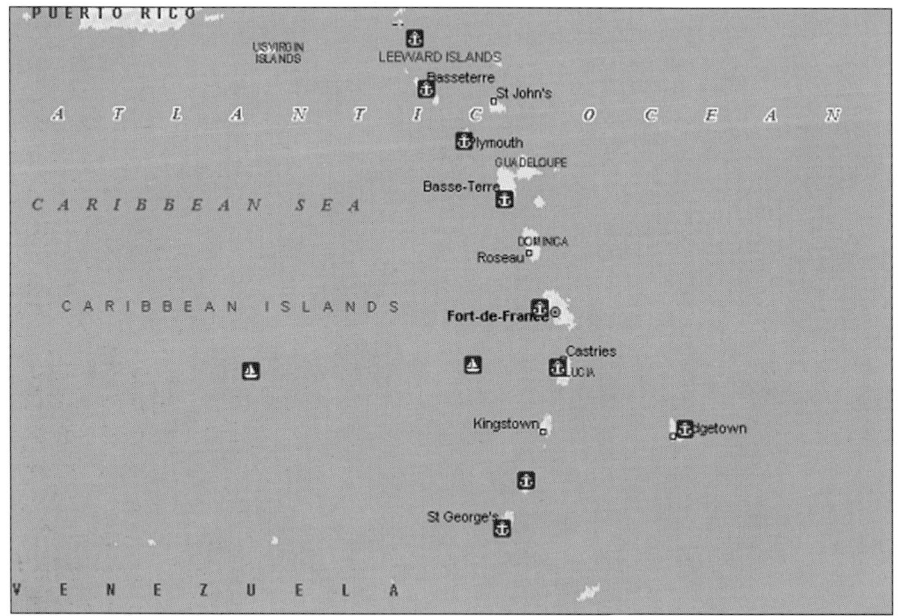

Islands of the West Indies.

the lee of the land, we lost the wind. At least we were able to have a good look at this steep-sided, pitted rock, five-hundred-and-seventy-five feet high, lying a mile-and-a-half off shore. The English dragged their cannons to the top of it using block-and-tackle and caused the French a lot of trouble until they were forced to surrender when they ran out of powder and shot. We used our motor to go down the lee of the island keeping close inshore, missing a lot of eddies and tiderips that cut the smooth water. After passing a couple of small bays we entered the main harbour. The size of the harbour and the town surprised me, and it took us quite a while to motor across the harbour against a strong current.

It was almost dark by the time we were off the old fort and sighted the familiar lines of the Norwegian fishing-boat. Dropping our anchor close by we took the two American women ashore without bothering about Customs, and rowed back to the fishing-boat to say hello to Gunner whom we had not seen since the Canary Islands. We cooked a good meal that night with Gunner supplying some wonderful, long loaves of French bread. Over our rum after tea we talked about our crossings. His was much the same as ours and he, too, took thirty-four days. Two other boats that he knew of were the 'Frisk' that took thirty-eight days, and the 'Four-Square' made a fast passage of twenty-eight days.

We decided to spend the day in Martinique, buy some bread to take back with us, and have a look around Fort-de-France. There is no comparison between the two islands. St Lucia is one hundred years behind. Although only thirty-six miles of water separate the two islands the difference is phenomenal. From what I can see it is the difference between the two ruling countries, France and England. France, like a good farmer, put back into the land a little of what it took out, but England has taken too much and given too little.

From what I saw of the people of Fort-de-France their disposition is much happier than the St Lucians and the prosperity of the island is much in evidence. While I was there, I did not see one person without shoes, all the people were well dressed and clean and drove their own cars. Many of the shops and stores there would match the smaller stores in New Zealand, and their prices under half of what is charged in St Lucia. We sailed at sundown from Martinique saying goodbye to Gunner who had decided to stop there and try fishing instead of going through to the Galapagos Islands. Once we were clear of the island the wind blew like hell but because there were only the two of us onboard we did not reef.

It was one of the wildest trips we ever experienced on the boat with strong squalls and rain; but sail, the old boat certainly sailed that night, with spray half-way up the mast and taking water from forward to aft for the first time. The return trip took seven hours and we were glad to drop anchor in the quiet of Castries Harbour. Duff was down at the boat at eight o'clock, dragging me out of my bunk ready for his day off, so very reluctantly I went back to the beach club.

There was a new guest there; a permanent one in charge of building a new hotel on the island, and he kept Duff and I on our toes – being first in the bar in the morning and last to leave at night. He was a Canadian, six-foot-four inches tall and had a capacity for drink to match his size. It did not matter what time he went to bed, at six o'clock sharp in the morning he was battering at the door waiting to get in. Duff would go to the kitchen and make his breakfast then put it into a plastic box because he never ate before ten. I would walk over to the bar, still half asleep, and pull six bottles of beer from the fridge, five for him and one for myself. With the five bottles lined up in front of him, he would drink them as if the bar was ready to close. Just in case he got thirsty before his six bottles of stout arrived at the job at dinnertime, I would pour another five bottles into a Thermos flask and away he would happily go to work. At four o'clock he would take up his position at the bar and what he would drink was anyone's guess. He might start off with a bottle of wine, switch to vodka and tomato juice, have a whiskey or two and then start on the liqueurs, always drinking doubles and sometimes trebles. With a short spell for dinner he would be back at the bar and into it again. I should imagine that he stayed in a perpetual state of semi-drunkenness. I know that he spent as much in one day as I earned in a week. I got so used to seeing him there that I would mop up around him as if he was a permanent fixture on the bar.

The brigadier and his wife were the next ones to charter the boat for the day to take them to a little bay along the coast. I sent a message to Bill telling him that a retired admiral was coming on board for the day. It certainly did the trick, because when I arrived the boat looked as if it was ready for an admiral's inspection; everything polished up and scrubbed clean. We took the boat alongside and picked up our passengers because the brigadier could hardly walk as a result of a stroke. There was less trouble than I expected and we got away under sail with an early start and a light wind.

We were lucky again with the weather as it was a beautiful, clear day with no rain, and going along in the lee of the island only a few hundred yards from shore, the water was like glass with just enough wind to move us along. It only took a few hours to reach the bay with its narrow entrances. Unless you knew it you could pass by and not guess what lay behind. The French did this in the days of the square-riggers when part of the English fleet hid in there as the French sailed by. Through the narrow entrance Marigot Bay opened up to form a small harbour. We headed for a sand spit jutting out in the centre covered with thick vegetation and palm trees. There was no need to anchor here as with ten feet of water close to the shore you could just jump ashore and tie up to a palm tree.

It was a pity that the brigadier could not go ashore, but he did not seem to mind too much. His wife produced a hamper that would have done justice to six men, but Bill and I managed to polish it off without any trouble. Ten bottles of beer were brought on deck and, knowing that he liked whiskey and his wife gin and tonic, we found a couple of bottles and some ice, and a really pleasant time was spent there in one of the quietest and most peaceful harbours in the islands. Taking the boat out of the harbour under sail we ran aground on a bank of soft sand but there was no trouble getting her off as Bill walked forward to lift the stern a bit, while I took a deep breath and went over the side and pushed her off.

On the way back the wind had freshened a little and the brigadier took the helm for a while, enjoying it very much, as he once owned his own boat in England. Close to the entrance of the harbour we started our motor as the wind was heading us off, and it was just after this we sighted the 'Topaz' with our friend the Rhodesian on board whom we left in Las Palmas waiting for his mast. He had dropped his sails and went down to start the motor only to find that it would not start. He was drifting close to the shore so I headed full speed towards him so he would not have to trouble putting his sails up again.

By the time we were close enough to throw him a rope his boat was a little too close to the rocks for comfort, but there was no trouble and we towed him into harbour. For the brigadier's wife it was the crowning end to a wonderful day and something she will talk about for a long time. To her it was a great adventure for not only did we save the boat from being smashed on the rocks, we undoubtedly saved old Ted from a watery grave. It is not often I have seen two people so old and yet so much in love, and the way they treated and fussed over each other you would have thought that they were still courting.

After putting our passengers ashore we anchored alongside the 'Topaz'. Old Ted looked much the same with his battered black hat on his head, no shave and, after thirty hours at the helm, he felt like a sleep. He brought his boat from Las Palmas to Barbados by himself and he, too, took thirty-four days. Gunner arrived in harbour not long after, from Martinique ready to slip his boat and do the bottom, so the three boats were together again. As it was Duff's day off I had to go back to the beach club while the three crews went ashore, plus two others off a thirty-footer bound for Australia. The rum flowed pretty freely that night.

Back at the beach club we got another charter: a young German-Canadian on holidays from working in a nursery in Canada. He was a quiet bloke, did not drink, smoke or swear and at twentythree had not slept with a woman, but we did not hold that against him as he was keen to learn to sail. After warning him what to expect and telling him that he would learn the hard way, he chartered us for a trip to the Grenadines for a hundred dollars US. With such a good excuse to get away from the beach club, I took off back to the boat to get things ready for the trip. Bill had been leading an ideal life back on the boat with the rum-shop girls coming on board and cooking his meals for him. I was not surprised to find three of them on board when I returned.

It was a bit hard to get the girls off the boat sometimes when there was work to do. They would arrive early in the morning after their night's work was finished and stand on the quay, waving and yelling until one of us would row over and get them. Sometimes they brought the food or we would give them the money to go and buy some from the market. With three of them in the dinghy, everyone working close by would stop and grin as we went past. Back on board they would make themselves at home. One would start cleaning and salting fish, another one would get my typewriter and, with my help, thump out a message to Duff at the club, another one with a more businesslike outlook would be on deck with the binoculars picking out prospective customers on the other yachts close by. None of these girls could read or write and as for carrying out a conversation with them, it was just not possible. I used to wonder how they could stay on board day after day, sometimes sitting for hours without talking or doing anything. That was until I saw how and where they lived: in broken-down shacks you would not keep fowls in, with no such thing as water laid on, no electricity, toilets unknown - all that went out of the window with the rubbish. Big holes were in the floors and bigger ones in the roof, so that when it rained everything had to be rolled up in a corner. If it was reasonably dry, then you perched on the top of the pile and hoped it did not rain too long.

There are hundreds of these shacks, all overcrowded, dirty and so rotten that they should have fallen down fifty years ago. There is water and electricity there alright, but when you get six or eight shillings a day in a place with a cost of living as high as New Zealand, you don't have much money for luxuries. To the girls who came on board it must have been quite a thing to be able to walk forward and use a toilet, to flick a switch on and listen to the radio and be able to go on deck in the sun. Then, of course, the blue bloods of the island, the rich people on their big yachts, would turn up their noses. These people think they are kings here, whereas back in their own country they would not be noticed. Yes they're rich and have a yacht; but mostly they got their money by keeping the people ignorant, with an inadequate school system and by exploitation of labour. When these people turned their noses up in the air I didn't give a damn. If the girls wanted to go on deck with just their brassieres on, they did just that. When the banana boat came into harbour and the crew went ashore the girls would disappear for a day or so. When they felt like it and were ready they came back on board again. Bill and Duff would take one or two of them to the pictures and sit in the balcony. Of course, there were always some looks, but it was O.K. if you were a black man and had half-a-million, then you could sit with a white woman. I was glad when the boat was ready, food on board and Jim came along from the beach club so we were able to sail and get away from the place for a while, out to sea where it is fresh and clean and there is no rottenness.

With Jim on board we gave him his first lesson; hauling in the anchor, which was not such an easy job for someone who did not know how to go about it properly. However, he managed to get the ninety-pound anchor up on our big, heavy chain covered in slime and, although he was blowing a bit by the time he was finished, he stood for a while looking at the mud on his hands then, to my satisfaction, he wiped them on the back of his pants like any good sailor. There was a lot more mud to join it by the time the trip was over, as we lifted and dropped the anchor over two-dozen times. We got under way with a good breeze that carried us out of the harbour and along the lee of the island until we passed the Pitons; two very high mountains with Soufriere Bay in the background. Then we were past the island and into the channel where we romped along with a strong wind and a good sea.

We lost the wind in the lee of St Vincent and it was not until twelve o'clock at night that we dropped anchor just off the jetty in Kingstown Bay. In the morning, we went ashore and had a look around. As we did not fly the quarantine flag no-one bothered us or came on board, so we set off at eleven o'clock for Bequia Island and after a good sail, entered the big bay at three in the afternoon. To me the big bay at Bequia is the most beautiful in all the islands, even its name, Friendship Bay. The bay is lined with white beaches and palms. The hills in the background were cleared of vegetation, but still enough there to give it a tropical touch. The little settlements around this big horseshoe-shaped bay were clean and tidy, the houses well looked after and painted.

Ashore there were plenty of flowers and hedges, small palm trees with sweet-drinking nuts and plenty of breadfruit trees, bananas and patches of yams. We bought a big bunch of bananas for twenty-five cents, but the locals refused to take any money at all for the drinking nuts, oranges and breadfruit. It was a change to be able to go and buy bread without having the hands of an old woman and skinny ragged children thrust in front of you, begging for a penny for bread. After a swim and tea it was a pleasure to sit on deck with a bottle of rum, while the boat rocked at anchor only yards from shore in the quiet of the evening.

We sailed at eight a.m., passing small islands all the way until we arrived at Union Island in the late afternoon. Another quiet anchorage with no towns or houses visible, it was a place with tall cliffs and coarse scrub. The only signs of life on the island were a couple of small fishing-dinghies pulled up in the shade and a mob of goats bleating high on the hillside, and that night we had the bay to ourselves.

We set off again early in the morning and once more had good wind across the channel but lost it again in the lee of Grenada. There is no doubt that this island is the prettiest in the whole group, and it took us three hours to run down the island to the main town, passing small bays and inlets, towns and villages, plantations of bananas, sugar-cane and coconut palms. On most of the bottom slopes of the high rugged, cloud-covered mountains, the land was cultivated and the patchwork of the crops was evidence of rich soil. The main town of St George was a lot bigger than I had expected and the harbour a good safe one where you could tie up to the wall. The Customs Officers wanted to know where our flag was when we arrived but there was no trouble with them. The two cases of whiskey we had on board had them scratching their heads for a while. They just could not understand why we had the two cases we had bought in England still on board.

That night we all went ashore to the pictures to see some wild-west show, but the yelling and screaming of the locals made it hard to hear anything at all. Next day we had a look around the town and bought some stores including three big steaks; the first that we had had for six months. We then took the boat around to a little bay up the coast and spent the day there, going ashore in the afternoon for a walk up a long valley with a small stream along its bed. Here every conceivable type of fruit and vegetable was growing, more or less in its native state. The people we met on our way saw that we did not go thirsty for the want of drinking-nuts. Judging by the reactions of some of the younger children it was the first time that they had seen a white man. Some would just stand and stare open-mouthed, others would roll their eyes and take off into the bush with the speed of a startled deer, and some of the younger ones, too petrified with fear to move, would just stand there screaming until we beat a hasty retreat around the bend on the track.

That night I cooked a meal that had the boys sitting back with contented looks on their faces and, after a couple of rums and coconut juice, we turned in and had a good night's sleep. In the morning there was not enough wind to take us out of the bay, but eventually Jim and Bill paddled her out with the dinghy oars and there we sat for two hours until a squall came up and took us clear of the island. From there the wind headed us off and we stood out to sea on a tack. We sailed all night and cut back towards land in the early morning; and what a pounding we took, beating to windward against the trades with strong winds and short, vicious seas.

It took us thirty hours to reach Union Island from Grenada and I was pleased to get into that sheltered bay once again. Jim took to the sea like a duck to water, was quick to learn and took his turn at the helm in the thick of it, never feeling sea-sick at all. We all had a bad half-hour fifteen miles out at sea when we got fish poisoning from a tuna we had caught the day before. We had some for tea that was quite alright and again for breakfast, but it must have gone off and it didn't take long for things to start to happen. Within ten minutes Jim looked as if he was going to die. All of his skin went red and blotchy and he started to itch all over. His eyeballs went red and he had a terrible headache. I was starting to get worried as I knew how long it would take us to get in, but he managed to get rid of the fish and in an hour he was feeling okay again.

I felt as if someone had hit me between the ears with a sledgehammer and, deciding to get rid of the fish, I had a good drink of salt water. However, my system probably thought that it was a new type of grog because nothing happened, and I not only had to put up with the fish but a belly full of salt water, too. Bill felt nothing at all and would have eaten a second helping if he could have got hold of it. It took me a while before I could enjoy a feed of fish after that. There were two other ships in the bay; a British warship (a frigate) and a seventy-foot Brixham Trawler, and what a fine ship she was with her tan sails and topmast. Both the crews were invited over to the frigate for a drink. This time we got as far as the wardroom and, after an hour of swapping stories and a few drinks, the captain stood up and said, "Well, goodnight", and that was that. I think he was a bit put out because no-one was taking any notice of him.

We sailed early the next morning, with the wind heading us off again and squalls most of the day, arriving at Cannon Island late afternoon. Next day was beautiful sailing weather, and we sailed into Friendship Bay at Bequia against a strong wind that heeled the boat over as Bill tacked and dodged around and between the schooners and fishing-boats anchored there. The boat must have looked good because we made

Americans on their yachts run for their cameras, and Jim stood open-mouthed as we came about with the bowsprit only feet away from some of the boats. We anchored just off the jetty in about ten feet of water and spent the rest of the day swimming and laying in the sun.

The next day we had strong winds but lost them in the lee of St Vincent. It was one of those days when you didn't mind just drifting along, only yards from shore in some places, watching the sea pound against the high cliffs or disappear into some cavern that it had cut over thousands of years. For most of the afternoon we just quietly moved along the coast until about four o'clock when we sighted a narrow opening, so narrow that at first we did not think we would be able to take the boat through. As we drew nearer we sailed over shallow patches of sand, and darker patches denoting reefs which at one time would have made me hold my breath as we passed over them. However, after passing over so many you get to be a fair judge of how much water is under the keel. Behind the entrance it opened up into a small, circular bay which at one time may have been a volcano in years long past. After sailing into the bay we dropped our anchor a hundred yards from shore, only to find the anchor and chain disappearing into unfathomable depths below. It was only after a lot of skinned knuckles that we managed to stop it and began the back-breaking job of hauling it all back on board. In the end we tied the stern to a palm tree and I walked the anchor out forward along the bottom of some boulders and bedded it so that we did not have to worry about any squalls that may come whistling through the hills during the night.

After a lot of hard sailing it was good to be in a place like this. At sea you think and dream of such a place but very seldom find it. Always there is something to spoil it, or it is not just quite right, but that night I was at peace both physically and mentally, a peace that is hard to find, that you sometimes know when you are with a woman you love. As the sun went down I wished it could stay a little longer so I could imprint in my mind the colours of the cliff with the green mat of creepers and vines hanging down close to the water, and remember the colours just as they were. A mob of goats browsed along the water's edge while the young kids played, stood and stamped their hoofs at each other. Birds burst forth in a flood of song, as if unwilling to give way to the coming darkness and, as the trees grew hazy, then fluffy, and the leaves melted into one, then the birds fell silent one by one. Before I knew it the moon was there; a big, full one that bathed the night with a soft light. The goats became vague shadows on the beach and the only sounds were the rustle of palm trees, the crickets singing their song of the night, and the wind as it whispered across the bay marking its passage and rippling the calm waters. When I finally turned in to sleep a dreamless sleep, I knew it would be a long time before there was another night and another place like this.

When we sailed in the morning we did not get any wind until we were out in the channel towards St Lucia, then the wind headed us off and we had to tack out to sea. It was not until eight o'clock that night that we managed to get into the harbour of Soufriere, after using our motor for three hours. We anchored very close inshore because of the deep water in the harbour. In the morning I was surprised to see what the second, biggest town on the island looked like. The bay itself was pretty and the two very, high mountains gave it a good background but there was little else; a few buildings and long rows of dilapidated houses and fishermen's shacks.

Before we sailed we spent a few hours ashore having a look around and cleared the harbour with a fair wind at twelve o'clock. We arrived back in harbour in St Lucia just before dark after a trip of five-hundred miles which had taken us twelve days. Back in the harbour I did not like the thought of returning to the beach club and finally came up with the answer.

Since we had a boat and Jim had a few lazy dollars, five hundred of them to be exact, we decided to have a bash at rum-running. At the rum shop where we drank ashore we were able to find out all we wanted to know and teamed up with a German who was doing a bit of smuggling himself, until he had the misfortune of being caught flat-footed with eighty cases of rum on the beach when his truck did not turn up.

Since he was out of business with his boat confiscated, he was willing to handle the shore side as long as we brought him back a hundred dollars worth of rum so he could start up a rum shop himself. Over a rum or two, with the chart spread on the table, we worked out the trip with a background of drunks, homosexuals and whores. Because no-one wanted to take the rum in cartons the first thing we had to do was get hold of thirty sacks. Since the market was the cheapest place that's where we headed and, when we asked for thirty, what a stir that caused. Women came from everywhere with sacks. Most of them had so many holes they would have made good fishing nets, so we had to sort them and shake the cockroaches out.

Nearly everybody in the market wanted to know why we wanted thirty sacks, and some of the answers we gave them were fantasies. At least it kept them quiet, but we gave up all hope of keeping our sack-

buying a secret. Whilst taking them back to the boat in a taxi we passed the Customs Officer and gave him an unconcerned wave, we hoped, while he eyed the bundle of sacks speculatively. That night, up the street, we were stopped by half-a-dozen people all wanting to know if we wanted more sacks. However, what really made us grit our teeth was when someone would lean out of a house and yell the same question while we were still a block away.

We waited eight days for the German to line up some banana-paper for us to wrap the bottles in and, when we got it, two rolls each three feet high, I wondered what we would tell people if they asked what we were going to use it for. With our money changed we had just under one thousand West Indian dollars and sailed on the fourth of February to Martinique where we stopped the night, went ashore in the morning and bought stores. Sailing at noon, we went along the western side of the island, passing more plantations which were watered by irrigation sprinklers, the first I had seen in these parts. We then passed the new town of St Pierre with the church steeple prominent in the foreground.

To the left of the town lay the mighty mountain which had erupted so savagely and violently in 1902, destroying the whole town and killing forty-thousand people before the sun had set that day. Buried forever was the town and its people under tons of ash and molten rock, leaving a lava bed to mark the place where people once lived, laughed and loved. The crews of the sailing ships that were on deck when the side of the volcano blew out were the lucky ones, as they would have died instantly. The superheated steam would have cooked their flesh and stripped it from their bones before a scream of terror could reach their lips. The dark clouds that were swirling and rolling around the hidden summit cast a shadow on the new town not too far away, sitting serene and peaceful in the warm sunshine.

Once clear of Martinique, we had good sailing until we came into the lee of Dominica. It took us all night to clear the island, cross the channel and then sail into the lee of Guadeloupe as the sun came up. For the rest of the day we battled our way along the island against head-winds and squalls and anchored in a little bay on the north-west end late in the day. Sailing early next morning the winds were strong and we kept off the coast a bit, passing Montserrat about six miles off. We had to reef down just before Nevis Island at twenty-four hundred. From there we had a good run to St Kitts and dropped anchor in the open harbour early in the morning.

Rum-smuggling, Saint Barthelemy.

Later in the day we went ashore and had a look around. Except for a high mountain in the centre of the island the rest of the land was flat and all cultivated, much of it under sugar cane. The harbour itself was shallow and all the schooners anchored there had to unload their cargoes into small boats and then row ashore. It was just on dark when we sailed out of the harbour and had a fair wind until midnight, when the wind headed us off as we entered the shallow water between the two islands. In no time there was a big sea running that threw the boat around like a cork. Bill and I managed to sleep through it all but Jim, at the helm, told us later that he was sure the boat was going to founder at any moment.

Because of the head-winds we did not think we would reach our destination as planned, but the wind changed and dawn found us off St Barthelemy, sailing over very shallow water, trying to work out which was the passage between the rocks that stuck up everywhere. Finally, we picked one of the three entrances and went in under motor, dodging around a rock known by the locals as Whale Rock. Only a foot of this rock showed and was hard enough to see in calm water; had we come in at night it would have been impossible.

I don't think any other island could surprise me as much as this one did. Coming up to the entrance, the harbour was more like entering a narrow river that wound back between low hills. Outcrops of rocks, red from the leaching of iron, stood thrust up like markers everywhere. The few buildings that made up the town were nestled along the waterfront, which was lined along its length with stone, and the quay walls there reminded me of Yarmouth, England. The remains of old stone buildings, built by the Swedes when they first settled there, were scattered around the hillsides. The most impressive of the ruins was a big hotel built over a century before. The inscription over the big, arched doorway was already obliterated, the windows empty, the roof gone, allowing the sun to shine through into the darkest corners. The weeds and small shrubs forced their way through the cracks in the stone floor and were growing as they did before the builders came. Although they are long gone and their names sunk into oblivion, the walls still stand as a credit to their workmanship and these, with the other ruins and the small log shacks with their shingled roofs, give the place a unique setting.

After tying up alongside I went to one of the three warehouses on the right bank, asked for the boss, and gave him an order for a hundred cases of rum and four of brandy, paid him the money and it was as easy as that. Some of the locals showed us where the deeper water was and gave us a hand to swing the boat around and haul it along the quay, and within fifteen minutes a truck arrived and dumped a load of rum alongside the boat. When we saw the size of the load we wondered where the hell we were going to put it, but it had to go on so we spat on our hands and got to work, and work we did, from ten o'clock until seven at night.

Jim cut the paper for wrapping the bottles, yards and yards of it, until he had blisters on his fingers, and then he cut some more. I wrapped them and Bill stacked them in the sacks. We worked like process workers on a bonus production, sweat pouring off us as we worked down in the little cabin stowing the sacks as they were filled, until slowly the boat was loaded forward to aft.

When we were finished, the only clear space on the boat was near the galley; a patch three feet by two. The toilet had three sacks in it, the sail locker four. Bill's bunk had two and there was another four on the floor. Four sacks went behind Duff's bunk, leaving Jim a foot to sleep on. The cabin was completely full of sacks standing on their ends so that we had to crawl along the top of them to get outside, and last of all was the cockpit. It had three sacks that almost filled it, and my bunk had another two. That took care of the whole load. Looking at the boat from the quay, it looked as if it was half swamped. The water-line had disappeared somewhere below the water and, in the shallow water, our keel was bumping on the bottom.

While we were busy loading, another boat came in for a cargo of grog, a big, West Indian schooner. The crew, a hard-looking lot, looked as if they were old hands at the game and they had their boat loaded about the same time as us. Their boat was also well down in the water by the time they had finished stacking the cases of rum and brandy. On top of that they loaded the boat with big kegs of white rum. They cooked their evening meal on a fire which they lit on the quay. Watching them in the twilight as the flames from the fire threw the light across their muscular torsos and expressionless faces, they squatted around the fire cooking the hocks of a young steer that was killed that day I couldn't help but think that they certainly added character to the place.

In the evening, quite a few of the locals came down for a yarn and to look at the boat. Many of them were descendants of the first Swedes – before they gave the island to the French on the condition that the island remained a free port. The people seemed to lead a quiet, unhurried life and I was sorry I did not have more time to have a good look around and meet more of the people. It is the only island of the Caribbean that I would like to go back and see again. When it was time to turn in it was a bit hard to find a place to lie down. Jim, of course, had the remainder of his bunk, I finished up stretched out on the chart table and Bill, like a wandering Arab, folded up a sail and disappeared into the night.

In the morning we sailed with a light wind and took the boat out of harbour and across the reef under the staysail alone. Clear of the island, we hoisted all sail and set our course for St Kitts. The boat was down by the head a bit but she moved along alright. At sundown we were off St Kitts and making good time, then the wind dropped and at dawn we were still off the island. The wind came up around nine o'clock, but from ahead, so we used our motor for a while. We only had four gallons of petrol on board and when we had used three of them we began to tack.

We lost the wind at sundown when we were between the islands of Nevis and Montserrat, and gave up all hope of getting back in time to deliver the grog as planned. For forty-eight hours we lay becalmed off the thousand-foot-barren rock, Redonda, and after the first twenty-four hours began calling it the Rock of Despair. The wind came up around nine the second night and we got underway. When we were close enough to the island for our petrol to last we started the motor, deciding to take the chance and go into Montserrat to send a telegram to the German and to get more petrol. Because of our load, we decided to anchor in a small bay away from the town and, having no chart of the island, we had to run down the island close to the shore looking for it.

It was one of those pitch-black nights when you could not see much further than the end of the bowsprit. Bill was up forward with our patent lead-line, "Duff's fishing line with the small axe tied on the end", and the way he was swinging it around his head before letting drive I wouldn't have been surprised if he came back holding an ear in his hand. With the booming of the surf and the flashes of phosphorescence as the waves pounded on the beach we had enough trouble feeling our way along and then, to make matters worse, a squall hit us bringing heavy rain, making the night blacker and drowning out all sound. No sooner had we got all sail down when the motor stopped, out of petrol, and we had to fight all our sail up again.

Fortunately the squall did not last long and we were able to see the lights of the town ahead. We must have missed the small bay in the dark and in the end, seeing a couple of dark objects in the water, we dropped anchor in about three fathoms half a mile from the town, and crawled thankfully down below. We were up at first light and could see no sign of the small bay. The two objects we had seen turned out to be buoys off the Shell depot. The jetty was a good quarter of a mile away and the first thing I looked for were any fast patrol boats that may have been tied up there, but there was not a fast boat in the bay.

Bill and Jim rowed ashore at six o'clock and landed at the jetty, while I waited on the boat getting things ready for a fast getaway. Bill arrived back two hours later with the petrol, leaving Jim on the wharf to answer questions and sweat a bit. Then it was my turn to start chain-smoking when he had to take the ship's papers ashore to the Customs Officers waiting on the wharf, who had suggested that we move the boat up. Of course, Bill tactfully refused, but he was not sure when he went ashore again that it would not be an order. Half an hour later I saw our dinghy pull away from the wharf with Jim and Bill in it, and by the time they got to the boat I had the motor started. The mainsail had been up all the time.

As soon as the dinghy was on board we got underway with the motor going full bore and all sails set, heading along the island towards Guadeloupe. We were ten miles off the island to seaward and the north point was abeam when the sun went down. Although we seemed to do a fair mileage during the night, a strong current against us reduced our speed so that at dawn the south end of the island was still ahead of us. Around nine we picked up a light wind from astern that blew all day and night so that we cleared Dominica and started to run down Martinique early morning. What moon there was had already left the sky and, in the inky darkness before dawn, we almost collided with a schooner running into the shore with no lights and painted black. At a guess, I would say she was going to put a load ashore herself.

On clearing Martinique, we had a good trip across the channel. We had hoped to arrive off St Lucia at night but, as there was nothing else for us to do, we crossed our fingers and ran the boat into the bay where Duff was working (using the lead-line all the way) and anchored about a hundred yards off the beach club. Leaving Bill and Jim on board I swam ashore with my clothes tied to my head, only to find that it was Duff's day off, so I had to go into town, find the German and let him know that we had finally arrived. I found him sitting in his empty bar drinking the profits so didn't bother to ask him how business was going. Although he was glad to see me he did not waste much time telling me how he had spent four hours sailing up and down the coast looking for us before he got our telegram.

As it was too late to organise anything for that night we decided to take the boat to Marigot Bay and wait for the German to arrange the transportation of the rum. It was dark when I arrived on board and we got underway. We arrived in the bay at midnight, tied up to a tree and had our first good sleep for a few nights. In the morning I got up when I heard voices close to the boat and went on deck to find a couple of West Indian fishermen staring at Bill's leg dangling over the side, while the rest of him was covered with a pile of sails. By the looks they gave me they probably thought that the leg belonged to a dead man and it wasn't until Bill got up that they went away.

In the calm waters of the bay the boat looked as if it was half swamped and more than one person passing by in boats said, "God damn, look at that boat. She sure must be heavy to lie that low in the water." The German arrived late in the afternoon, said it was as good as any place to unload and told us to take the boat across to the other side of the bay.

I was not too keen on the place he had picked to unload, as there was a hotel not too far away and the moon was getting around to half full, also there was another yacht anchored close by. However, just on seven o'clock we heard the truck coming and I went over the side to push the boat off. The night did not start well. I landed one foot right on top of a sea urchin, broke the standing high-jump record and came down squarely on another one. With two feet full of spikes I was far from happy. Then, while we were getting the bags ready, we found that quite a few of the bottles were leaking, from their tops coming loose, so that the boat smelt like a rum shop in no time.

We ran the boat right inshore, I jumped over the side and was lucky this time. Jim passed the bags up from the cabin and Bill put them on my shoulders. As each sack weighed over a hundred pounds I sank down a foot in the sand and it was quite a job to take them ashore. By the time they were all on land I felt that I had done a hard day's work. The truck was parked on the road a fair way from the beach and, with the two men who had come with the truck, five of us started to take the load up to the road. The narrow track coming from the beach was suddenly full of hurrying figures, bent almost double as they tripped over a root, or the clink of a bottle. Sometimes a figure would appear in a patch of moonlight that filtered down through the trees, but it would be gone before you could see who it was.

By the time the last sack was on the truck there was not much room for any more and I was glad to hear it start back along the road to town. At least the rum was off the boat and that was the main thing. I don't know where the expression rum-running came from but it certainly fitted that night. We did all the running from the truck to the beach and the rum ran too; bottles of it, down my head and over my back and chest. My shorts were soaked with it. The three of us could be smelt fifty feet away, and when I lit my first cigarette I did it very warily and waited until I was near the water. We took the boat back across the bay and tied up to a palm tree. Down below there seemed to be an enormous amount of room and the old boat, relieved of its burden, floated much more lightly.

We sailed at first light in the morning, so the people around would not notice our sudden rise in freeboard, and cleaned and scrubbed the cabin out on our way to Castries. We dropped anchor in our old spot at eleven o'clock, the whole trip taking thirteen days. We had no trouble with the Customs. They came on board but did not bother to have a look around. That night Bill and the German were racing around the town delivering rum as if it was bottles of milk.

The money from the rum came in slowly and after three days we had enough to go over to Martinique to buy stores for our trip. Jim was coming with us and the German also wanted to come across and do some business. The night before we left a retired American reporter came down to the boat wanting to go across with his wife and a young English couple. Although it was far too many for the boat we did not want to miss out on the money and agreed to take them across for fifty American dollars. In the morning we had the boat alongside at six o'clock. The German arrived with some bloke who was bumming his way around the islands, so we let him come with us for five dollars. Sweeney and his party arrived not long after, all decked out in sun hats, looking cheerful and happy.

With nine on board we sailed out of the harbour. At the best of times there was not too much room on board, and it was like an obstacle course trying to work the boat, be polite all the time, saying "Excuse me" as you moved everyone around the boat like figures on a chessboard, and saying "Sorry" as you kicked someone or stood on their hand. As we cleared the harbour one look at the sea told me that we were in for it. There were waves three feet high where usually it was dead flat and for the first half an hour while we were a little in the lee, it was alright. Sweeney and his wife, who had owned their own boat, knew what to expect but the English couple had never been to sea before on a small boat.

As we cleared the island we started to get the strong wind and bigger seas. Up until then we had not shipped any water on board and everyone was remarking what a dry boat she was. The Sweeneys and the English couple were sitting in the cockpit, their straw hats on, smoking and talking, when one of those sneaky waves, a beauty it was, too, curled up and dropped into the cockpit. Their hats became shapeless pieces of straw that flopped down around their ears, soggy cigarettes dangled from their mouths and they sat for long seconds with stunned looks on their faces. It was not long after this that things began to happen.

The German was already on his back, looking like death warmed up. Then the Englishman's wife went down below and laid on a bunk, looking like a corpse, and did not move for the rest of the trip. The bloke going around the islands was the next to feed the fishes then sat on deck, hanging onto the main boom, eyes closed, swaying with the roll of the boat, and seemed to be unaware of where he was or what was going on.

The Englishman lasted fairly well before he went to the side, and he did it so quietly and obscurely that I almost missed him. Then, showing that true British spirit, he sat quietly down in the same place, never once complaining, always being polite, and took all the sea and the sky could dish out. Sweeney never left the deck, only to fill his pipe with some foul mixture of tobacco which he smoked continually, and seemed to enjoy the trip. His wife, although there was not much of her, put up with more than most men would have, sitting in three inches of water most of the way, taking all the spray and wind right in her face as well as the rain that came in squalls.

It was a fast trip across the channel but we lost a lot of time crossing the bay to Fort-de-France against the current, and it was not until late in the day that we pulled into the wharf. The Customs then descended upon us and the fun began. It took two hours to clear things up and it wasn't until after dark that the group of tired and bedraggled passengers was allowed to go to a hotel. For myself, I could not understand what all the fuss was about. I felt a bit left out as I was unable to understand or speak one word of French. I would have liked very much to join in the argument and after watching all the hand waving, the shoulder shrugging and red faces until I got tired of it, I ambled off to see Gunner on his fishing-boat which was tied up around the corner.

He had done a lot of work on the boat since I had seen it last, and he was almost ready to start fishing. The longline lay ready up forward and he was just finishing the fish-hold after relining it with fibreglass and plywood for the ice he will have to carry as an insulation against the heat. The cost of the job almost broke him and he and his son had been living on a starvation diet for over a month, having just enough money for one trip. If they did not catch any fish they were finished. We took our boat alongside his later on and I cooked a good meal for the six of us. Quite a job on our little stove.

Although we went to bed early, with the grinding of hulls together and the mosquitoes, none of us had much sleep that night. We were in town at eight o'clock and only finished collecting the stuff we had bought at four in the afternoon. That night everyone went ashore for a meal while I stayed and talked with Gunner. We had taken the boat around and tied up behind a banana-boat and when she pulled out at ten o'clock, going full speed ahead, she threw our boat around like a matchbox in a stormwater drain. Only the four lines I had out forward and two aft held her from going back on the bows of the fishing-boats tied up behind us.

Just as I was ready to go to bed I was told to move as a very big banana-boat was coming in early in the morning. So around I went and tied up alongside Gunner again. I did not have any sleep that night. Around three o'clock in the morning, a barge loaded with tons of bananas caught our bowsprit and broke our forward line. Two hours after that two big fishing-boats tied up outboard of us to let the banana-boat in and we had to spend most of the time until eight o'clock fending them off as they put a terrific strain on our timbers. At eight-thirty our passengers arrived, all looking fresh and healthy. The English couple had thought about flying back but decided against it, and as soon as they were on board we cast off our lines and started back.

Gunner and his son watched us go for the last time and I was sorry I would not be able to go fishing with them as I had hoped. They had certainly lost a lot of weight since we first met them in Spain. With their hair cut short as it was, they looked as if they had just come out of a concentration camp.

The trip over was rough enough but it was a picnic compared with the trip back. We got the first of it as we cleared the island and had to reef down, and then half-way across we had to put another reef in. No-one was sick on the return trip, as those who were not sure took sea-sick tablets before we left. We took a fair bit of spray on board, even with the reduced sail, as the wind went as high as force six in the squalls. The waves were making up a bit around the centre of the channel. Sweeney said they were close to thirty feet, and I figured he ought to have something for his money, so did not tell him they were only around half that size. The Englishwoman spent most of her time staring into Bill's and my face as we sat at the helm, looking, I think, for any sign of fear. When she would see none she would settle back until the next big wave loomed up and filled her mind with doubt. Her husband took it quite well, but was almost pathetic the way he lifted his head and stared towards land as if it was his last hope. Then the spray and water would hit him and he would drop his head almost between his knees in submission to the sea.

We used our motor coming into harbour and in the calm water everyone picked up a bit. Even the German, who had moaned most of the way back, shut his mouth for a while. When we disembarked them Sweeney told us he would bring the money down in the morning, which goes to show that anyone who pays for such a pounding is nuts, even a little bit more so than those who do it for pleasure. It was five o'clock when we anchored and Bill and I did not bother about food. We just turned in and slept for twelve hours.

It was another three days before we finally got squared-up for the rum. The total loss was just over a hundred bottles due to leakage, breakage, stolen and drunk. Since we did not know who was robbing who there was nothing we could do about it, but the loss of two hundred BWI dollars was quite a setback to our food supply. Duff by this time was becoming a prominent figure around town, always drunk on his day off, and I had a standard answer for people coming up and telling me about some episode in which he was involved, saying, "Yes, that would be him!" Among the stories we heard were that he was asleep on the lawn of the bank at eight o'clock in the morning, having a fight with someone outside the post office, sitting on a bollard on the wharf with his shirt hanging off him, kicking down his girlfriend's door, and punching her in the eye outside a rum shop. The German would give him rum on the slate and, when he started to make trouble, give him five dollars to drink somewhere else. There was no doubt it was time he got back to sea again.

With the boat ready to sail and all the supplies on board we waited for Duff to finish up the week at the club. Jim decided to finish his tour by plane as it was already paid for, then fly back to Canada and start work at the nursery again. I should imagine that he will find it pretty dull after being so long with us. When he left he swore like a Queensland drover, could bend his elbow with the best of us and toss back a beer like a Woolloomooloo wharfie, was right at home serving behind the bar in the German's rum shop, and he had the best load of clap that I had seen for many a day.

Duff arrived back with some terrible tales to tell us of the goings-on at the beach club and soon settled down on board again. The last night we all went ashore to a little rum shop not far from the boat. It was easy to find. The music from the jukebox throbbed out across the water like a giant heartbeat, as it did the first night. We followed the sound over the big timbers, through a boat-yard, down a muddy road that led from the dump, kicking squealing pigs out of our way, and passed the wrecks of cars, every one of them the home of the people living in them, including a glass-sided hearse from which a big pair of feet protruded (the owner slept under the small cross with RIP written across it that was still standing a little crooked on the roof).

Alongside the road the backwash of the bay lapped across a mud flat, the water almost reaching the first of the shacks there built on the mud and rubbish, so that they looked like flotsam that had been thrown up by the sea. Ahead the road separated two rows of tightly-packed shacks, the light from their oil-lamps showing briefly through the shutters on the windows and the cracks in the walls.

On the footpath where all the cooking is done the coals from the evening meal still glowed in the small, earthenware fireplaces, and incredibly skinny dogs nosed around for something to eat, baring their teeth as we passed, their growl lost with the sound of the music that was getting louder and louder. A square of light shone out of the doorway of the bar. The group around the jukebox was waiting for someone with five cents to punch another record. A couple of West Indians shuffled around the floor, eyes closed, limbs twitching spasmodically in a dance that their forefathers would have done around a fire long ago. Some of the crews from the schooners sat around the tables, drinking rum and smoking cigarettes that they bought one at a time. A couple of homosexuals danced together in the shadows, no-one taking any notice of them.

From the bar, a figure reeled away, hitting the wall, to stand there incapable of moving as if he were in a trance. One look and we knew that he had been drinking white rum. Duff and I tried it once, just once. After that we called it the white death and left it alone. Behind the bar stood a gigantic man whose bulk dwarfed everything around him. His forearms resting on the bar were the biggest I have seen on any man and he waved a hand, in greeting, that was the size of a dinner plate. Standing at the bar the music was so loud and penetrating that it seemed to be part of you – seemed to throb inside your head – and it was a relief to get our rum and ice and go out to the beer garden with the soft lights and where the music lost some of its power.

There was no-one in the garden. Some nights it was like that. Here we came night after night when we were in harbour to sit, to talk, listen and learn; where we could relax and drink our rum and see what the night brought, because the people who came here were many and varied. Politicians would argue for hours as if they were in the House, becoming so excited they would jump up and stomp around the cement floor, banging their fists into their palm or on the table to make their point. Captains of schooners and rum-runners would come here at the end of a trip. One fellow with a black beard who had sailed in the Caribbean for twenty years, knew every rock and shoal like the palm of his hand and was always laughing, would stand in the centre of the tables, glass held high, proclaim all seamen as brothers and the rum would flow like water.

'Old Sex,' as everyone called him, would wander in and have his flask of rum. He always dressed with coat, vest and tie and would tell everyone about the hundred-and-forty-two virgins he had slept with, noting their names and ages methodically in a notebook. Once he was worth half-a-million pounds but wasted most of it and one of the two big fires in the town finished him. Now he lives in a shack that even the pigs walk around.

James was by far the most interesting person to drink there. He was a tall man with a fine physique, and as he stepped through the doorway into the dull light it was as if he were a prophet who had just stepped out of the pages of the Bible. He was a stevedore and when he managed to get a couple of days work he would end up on the rum. He was self-educated and his thirst for knowledge was unquenchable. In his own way he was an intellect, and the more he read, learnt and saw, the more disillusioned he became. He would talk on any subject until he got drunk, then he was a different person and stark, raving mad. He would stand up in the centre of the tables and rave on for hours with eyes blazing and the strong features of his face portraying his every emotion, so that no words were needed. It was all there to see: the hate, the love and tenderness, the anguish, and the seeking as he stood there with his short, goatee beard, battling with something inside him. He made a striking figure and his mad laughter would ring out into the night.

From time to time girls would drop in; very seldom in ones and twos, usually always in a pack, like wolves, going from bar to bar hunting for men. It was pathetic to watch them when some of the crews of the banana-boats were in the bar. Always there were three times as many girls as men. Some would not even try, just sit down with a sigh and stare into space, the hopelessness on their faces. Some, like the pretty girl of sixteen, would sit and watch the others dance, almost getting up to join in, then the animal look would come on her face as she remembered the terrible disease she had and, although it was men that gave it to her, there would be no more men or dancing until it was gone. Even after six months of treatment and needles it was still there and would probably kill her.

Many of the white men working in the town came here when they wanted a night out because here there was no-one to point the finger at them. No-one would know and they could still mix with the snobs and talk about the ignorant savages over a pink gin, or some man who just didn't give a damn, or who was unlucky enough to be caught lowering the white man's precious prestige. Occasionally the chief minister, the ministers and town officials would find their way down the narrow streets, past all the broken-down shacks, not to see the conditions in which their people were living, but into the back bar to drink and raise hell, until half of them were asleep and the other half would be grouped around some woman whose virtue, of course, would be above reproach. I hope the saying "What goes around comes around" is true.

The Norwegians liked to boast that they were the only gunners on the whale catchers, but in this bar I met a small, wiry West Indian, who not only hunted the small, faster whale, but made his own gun, too. I was interested enough to go and have a look at the boat he hunted in and found a worm-eaten, open, twenty-foot boat with some pipes stuck up forward for the gun. His secret was in preparing the charges which only he had so far perfected. He made these up with just the right amount of black powder and had three in a set: one for close range, one for middle and one for far away. In case the whale should turn on the boat he smoked a cigarette and kept a stick of dynamite with a short fuse ready in his hand. This he would throw at the whale and stun it. I don't know what would have happened if his cigarette went out. I could not bring myself to ask him.

When I met him he had just finished making a new gun, so I went along one day to have a look at it. By his reputation I had expected quite a complicated gun but, when I saw it I could only shake my head. The barrel was a piece of two-inch water-pipe about four-feet long. On the end of this was a reducing socket and a plug with a hole bored through for the striker – a quarter-inch bolt, sharpened to a point, with a locknut. The spring of a doorstop gave it the striking power, helped along by a piece of tyre tube. A rough stock finished the model and would have broken any collarbone had it been fired from the shoulder. I refused a practical demonstration, thinking of a backfire, and bought him a rum every time I saw him for having the guts to fire the thing, let alone hunt the small whales. While I was there I saw one of the whales he had caught being loaded on a truck to be taken to the market and sold as meat.

I cannot remember who was in the bar the last night we were there. I think there was a little more white rum added to our bottle than usual. I know we were the last to leave and the big fellow guided me gently through the door and over the doorstep that seemed to be three feet higher than when I went in. The three of us found our way back to the boat without capsizing; a thing that always amazed anyone watching, and that had been a mystery to us since we started the trip.

In the morning we put the last of our fresh supplies on board, took on our water and rigged our spinnakers, booms and sails while we were alongside. Just as we were ready to go the wind dropped and we had to start our motor. We then hoisted our now-tattered New Zealand flag for the benefit of the Australian yacht, 'Homeward Bound' of Sydney, that had just arrived in the harbour and gave them a rally as we passed with our sails flapping, rolling like a barrel as we made our way out of the harbour and into the light winds outside. We were all glad to be on our way again. I don't think that one of us looked back.

Chapter Ten

St Lucia to Panama

We had no sleep for the first couple of nights until we got used to the rolling again and moved along with the light winds for the first week. Although the sea was full of plankton we caught no fish. Three boats passed fairly close to us so we put up our light every night. The current gave us a surprise by pushing us fifty-three miles north in two days, whereas no current showed on the chart and we were not able to get our 249 tables for longitude sights. We were still working with dead-reckoning and latitude sights, and after two days of very light winds and flat, calm seas we decided to hail the first boat we saw and get a check on our position.

When the wind came up it was from the north-west so we bent our new red mainsail, used one of the spinnakers for a headsail and, with this light canvas, we had a fair turn of speed. Then the wind swung around again and we ran under spinnakers once more. On the ninth day out we sighted another ship, a tanker, which turned out to be the 'Paul Piggott' from Monrovia. Her course would bring her to pass close to us so we took out the signal flags and hoisted the flags JG 'I wish to have personal contact with you' and the flags LEK for 'position'. The ship came up, passed us at a thousand yards and kept right on going.

By this time we had our sails down and the motor started. As she went past with no sign of stopping, we stopped the motor, hauled down our flag, and up went our sails again. The three of us then spent the next five minutes making very uncomplimentary remarks on the parentage of the

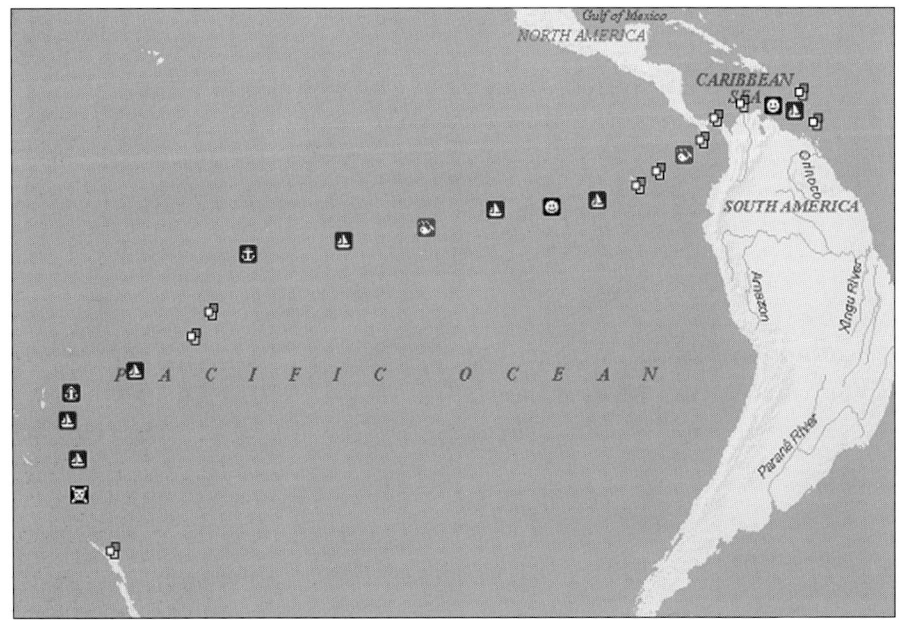

West Indies through Panama to New Zealand.

captain, and if the ship had been any closer our language would have blistered the paintwork on her sides. Then about a mile away she suddenly made a turn and came back towards us. By the time she reached us we were once more under sail. The captain came on the wing of the bridge and was more interested in finding out our nationality than anything else, but as soon as Duff came on deck holding up our flag like a standard bearer, he was satisfied. Shouting through a megaphone he gave us our position. We waved, shouted our thanks, and got underway again, while he circled around our stern. I thought he wanted to get our name but instead she came in alongside us, much too close, with the crew from the cook down, lining the rail. There was quite a swell running and we were rolling pretty badly. Seeing this wall of steel getting closer we went into action and it must have been quite a sight for the crew.

Bill hauled the spinnakers down, in case we caught our boom, Duff dived below like a madman to switch on the water and petrol, while I tore up the floorboard at the bottom of the cockpit to crank the motor. Over my shoulder I could see the ship's side getting closer and closer to our boom. The wash from the bow and the propeller was throwing us around like a cork. Everything around the cockpit kept falling into the bilge as I tried to crank the motor, so there was a continuous stream of plastic buckets, plates and brushes flying through the air from the cockpit down into the cabin. The motor which usually started with one or two cranks refused to turn over, even though I was winding so fast that we would have been doing around two knots if it had been in gear. Duff suddenly remembered he had forgotten to turn on the petrol and literally dived down through the hatch. The motor started while he was on the way back up, catching his toe in the flywheel, and he arrived on deck dancing around like a Fijian firewalker.

As the motor roared under full throttle I remembered I had locked the gear lever away. With no time for anything else I threw myself down and, with my head resting in the bilge, managed to push the four inches of lever in with my two hands, while my legs swung around in mid air above the cockpit. In gear the boat shot forward faster than it had ever done, our boom less than ten feet from the ship's side. Closer still were our mast spreaders that rolled in, almost touching the guardrail at the stern. As if we did not have enough trouble one of the spinnakers dropped into the sea and, with the speed we were going, it soon filled with water, bending the spinnaker boom as if it were a bamboo fishing rod, with Bill fighting and clawing like a wild man trying to get the sail out of the water.

The captain, unaware of just how close we were or what the wake of a ship like his does to a small boat like ours, gave us a cheery wave, turned the ship around and steamed off while the three of us surveyed our battle scars. Duff was nursing his toe, Bill looked at his broken fingernails and I gingerly fingered the bruises along my backbone. The day did not end too badly because Duff caught an eighteen-pound tuna towards sundown, and that night the wind started to blow up strong. It continued for four days and although the seas were fairly high they were long and regular. Sometimes at night the boat was like a mad thing, pitching and tossing, throwing Duff clean out of his bunk, going along like a horse with the bit in its teeth and wildly surging down the waves in a flurry of foam.

On the fifth day, after a few sleepless nights, we got up around eight o'clock to find a group of low islands dead ahead, right on our course, three miles away. Already we had one on our port beam and lost no time in getting our spinnakers down, thinking of what would have happened if the night had been a couple of hours longer. We put up our fore-and-aft sails and ran along the coast of Panama which showed in the distance behind the islands.

That night we sighted the light off Panama and started to run into the first of the shipping. All night we ran in towards the canal. The 'Southern Cross' passed us like a floating town early in the morning – only altering her course when she was close enough to see that we were under sail. At nine o'clock we passed through the narrow entrance of the mile-long breakwaters built of huge, stone blocks that looked as if they had been flogged from the pyramids in Egypt.

Chapter Eleven

Panama Canal

We anchored off one of the piers, well out of the way of all shipping, and waited for Customs. American organization was evident with well-laid-out piers, big warehouses, and ships everywhere – some anchored, others coming or going or being pushed around by pint-sized tugs. The place looked like the square in Christchurch on Friday night. Some officer finally arrived on board with a big, shiny badge on his shirt and a bag with insecticide, a tape and a pile of forms that would give anyone writer's cramp just looking at them, but he sat down and filled them all in for us then measured the boat for canal charges. He took the measurement from the tip of the bowsprit to the end of the bumpkin and gave us the surprising length of thirty-eight feet. This made no difference to the cost, which worked out to $3.20.

Our dinghy as usual was leaking like a sieve and, as the charge was $10 just to be taken over to the Customs office, we tried a few unsuccessful attempts with cans lashed around the sides and wedged under the seat, but even with Bill bailing and rowing, the dinghy sank until he was up to his chest in water. As we were not allowed to take our boat into the wharf we had to anchor again near a fishing-boat and borrow their longboat. Once we had our clearance we motored around and tied up to a buoy at the yacht club, the trip from the West Indies taking fourteen days.

The yacht club was the best that we had been to; hot water in the showers for the first time since we had left New Zealand, a good, quiet anchorage to work on a boat, and everything you could want to buy, if

Panama Canal.

you had the money. I've got to hand it to the Americans; they sure have living down to a fine art, everything so easy and simple, makes them soft I think but they certainly know how to take it easy. Duff disappeared ashore late in the afternoon and arrived back next morning looking sorry for himself.

The only other boat waiting to go through the canal was a fifty-foot Colin Archer. It was a magnificent boat, originally a North Sea rescue boat, with her bottom sheathed with iron for the ice and a powerful motor for towing. The young American who was taking it to the States offered to tow us through the canal with him and save us the long run under our own motor. I had hoped to go up the coast to Oporto and pick up a brand-new canoe Jim from Canada had left there for us. He had no way of picking it up and, although it was worth three hundred dollars, we did not have the time or the finances to make the trip. For the next two days we never stopped. We had decided to put most of our money into stores to last for the remainder of the trip to New Zealand, and the three of us walked our feet off chasing up food, charts and petrol – and we also had to see the Ecuadorian consul.

Food was fairly expensive to buy and the charts set us back more than we had hoped, so we were not able to afford any Pacific pilot books. The petrol we could get the other side of the canal through the yacht club. The visa was our only snag. If it cost more than $10 we would have gone direct to the Marquesas. We had heard quite a few tales about this consul. If half we had heard was true, he would make Ned Kelly look like a choirboy. Duff and I dressed up in our best clothes, which by this time did not make us look as if we had much money, and fronted up at his house. At first we did not get on very well. He looked us up and down as if we were a couple of worms, probably deciding there was no profit to be made out of us. He was not very helpful at all and, since we could not understand each other, I was forced to retreat. I found the first bloke on the street who could speak English and Spanish and fronted him again. This time we found out what we had to do. I don't know how many trips we made from the consul's place to town, about four or five, all on foot. Bill joined the fray later on and after eight hours of foot slogging we got our visa to the Galapagos Islands for $3.30. This was not too bad since the 'Hope', a boat of the same size just ahead of us, paid over $20.

We had to pay for a radiogram to Ecuador and I thought we were beaten when we were asked for $8 until he explained that it would get there in an hour. I have never seen a man's eyebrows lift so high as the Western Union man behind the counter as I leant over and said "Listen mate, the bloody speed we'll be going, you could send it by pigeon post". In the end we sent it for $4.

The next morning, with all our papers in order, the pilot came on board and we slipped from the buoy and motored slowly away from the yacht club on the old French Canal towards the first lock.

Our pilot was a nice enough fellow but one of those Americans who just could not relax. When we told him that the average speed of our boat was four knots he just sat and groaned, but was a little happier when we told him that Will's boat, the 'Sea-snake', would take us through. Even so, he had us motoring along at full speed against the current so that we had to wait at the first lock a half hour until we could enter it. A big merchant ship went in first then the 'Sea-snake' and, using his big towing hawsers, tied up bow and stern alongside the wall. We tied up outboard of him with plenty of tyres along our side and our lines, which were much too small, looked like fishing-lines against his hawsers. A big, powerful motor-boat tied up against the wall on the other side, then the lock gates closed and the water began to rise.

We had expected quite a current in these locks but nothing like the swirling water that rose up – as if we were in a giant cauldron – and plucked and threw us about like a piece of driftwood. Will's boat took all the weight of the two boats on his lines and was thrown in against the wall. Even with his big motor to help him his bowsprit took quite a knock, and it was only because his boat was so solid that he suffered no damage. Even with our treble lines I thought they would part as our rope stretched and the fibre started to give. They could not have taken much more when the current slackened off. The big motor-boat broke her stern line and by using her two powerful motors managed to keep herself off the wall.

In the next lock we tied up astern of the merchant ship. I should have remembered the banana-boat in Martinique, but I was too busy handling lines, not only on our own boat but Will's also. The current was much the same as the first lock, heeling us well over. The merchant ship went full ahead, the water boiled up in front of us, and the only thing we could do was stand there and hold our breath. It was as though a giant hand was slowly pushing us over until our gunnel was jammed under the rubbing strake of Will's boat and one of our bowsprit stays almost pulled out. Then as the merchant ship drew ahead we were sucked out from the wall until the hawsers on the 'Sea-snake' began to twang, but by using his motor he was able to hold both boats against the force of the current. The pilot on our boat began to abuse the pilot on the merchant ship, shouting across the water and waving a clenched fist. He had remarkable lung-power and did not draw a breath or repeat himself once, until he was so red in the face I thought he was going to explode. When he had calmed down he told us to make a claim for damages but there was really nothing we could not fix up ourselves.

The next lock was not quite so bad and when we had passed through this one we had been lifted eighty-five feet to the level of the lake. There we picked up the tow rope from the 'Sea-snake' and he started to tow us through twelve miles of lake which was bordered by thick jungle and had numerous small islands along the way. Dead branches of the taller trees that were once jungle before it was flooded still showed above the water. The passage through the lake did not take long. With its four-foot propeller the 'Sea-snake' did not feel the tow at all, and our old boat moved through the water faster than she had ever gone before, most of the time doing eight knots. It was a bit hard on the helm sometimes but it was worth it as our bow wave curled up just below the gunnels.

Just as we reached the 'cut', as it is called, one of the belts broke on the 'Sea-snake' and we took over the tow for a while just to keep steerage way until he got his motor going. Our pilot started to get worried about that time and insisted on full speed. I don't know what he thought he was in, but our full speed with the 'Sea-snake' in tow was two knots, and our motor was hot enough to fry eggs on in fifteen minutes. We managed to tow him about a mile through the 'cut' before his motor was ready and looking back I could see his bow wave at least two inches high.

With the 'Sea-snake' in front again, the trip through the 'cut' did not take long and there were some very surprised looks on the faces of the officers of a merchant ship as we passed them, tow and all. The 'cut' must have been quite a job when it was being built, blasted through solid rock at a depth of around fifty feet. Further on near the continental divide, that is where the canal started to drop towards the Pacific, big, earth-moving equipment was being used to widen it; bulldozers, scoops and cranes shifting tonnes of rock and dirt. A bit different to the Suez Canal, where hundreds of workers are doing the same job with baskets, picks and shovels.

Slipping our tow as we neared the first of the canals to drop us down, we went ahead under our own motor to enter the lock with our pilot. 'Full Ahead Cassidy' as we were now calling him, was standing up and shouting orders as if he were taking a battleship in. As usual he had us full ahead where I would have had us dead slow and as we came up to the lock wall I was wondering what he was going to do, but followed his orders, "port your helm", that headed us straight for the wall. Then, at ten yards, going full ahead, he shouts "full astern". Now on a tug or a bigger boat you can do things like that, but on our boat full astern did not get a chance to even start to slow her up.

We hit hard while the pilot stood there with his mouth moving like a fish out of water. Luckily the bobstay took most of the shock and we rode up on it until our bowsprit was jammed on the timbers at the top of the wall. No real damage was done and we were able to push our boat off. This did not worry our pilot who, of course said it was my fault. All his orders were still "hard this, hard that" and the only speed he knew was full. I was glad when we were in the last lock and the big gates swung open, giving us a glimpse of the Pacific water beyond, then we were through even before the gates were fully opened and, picking up the hawser from the 'Sea-snake', we were on our way again, the gateway to the Pacific behind us.

As our motor was starting to make a few unusual noises Duff decided to oil it and grease the nipples, switching it off to do so, and it just refused to start when we got to the yacht club. Never have I heard a man get so wild over nothing as our pilot. To him it did not matter about the motor. All he wanted to do was to get off the boat, even though the trip had taken us eight hours instead of the sixteen or more it would have taken under our own power. He raved on like an idiot and wanted to take us to a buoy with a pilot boat, a matter of a few hundred yards, at the cost of $10. We told him flatly "NO" and suggested anchoring. To this he yelled "RIGHT", dropped the anchor as if we had it all ready to let go instead of having to unlash it from the deck, mount and tie the stock, remove floorboards for the chain and then get it ready over the bow. While we were doing this he twice tried unsuccessfully to tie a knot that would hold to a line from the pilot launch so we could be held against the current. No sooner was our anchor on the bottom and he was gone. We were glad to see the last of him. Some of these pilots may be the best in the world on big ships, but on small boats they are lost. They just have no idea.

After changing the spark plugs the motor went without any trouble, and hauling up our anchor we motored around looking for a buoy. In the end we tied up alongside the 'Sea-snake' which was a mistake because we celebrated our arrival in the Pacific a little too strongly and loudly. I think everyone in Panama heard us. It started off well enough with the guitar thumping away and Maori hakas were done on the deck with the harpoon. After several hours anyone with any sense turned in, but not Duff and I. We were still watering our brandy with vodka at dawn. Remorse having set in by then I went to bed to escape the sun, and when I woke up the man with the hammer was at work once again in my head.

The next day the 'Sea-snake' sailed for the U.S. and, before he left, Will gave us the sight reduction tables 249 that we had been trying to get since England for our longitude sights. Looking around for a place to paint the bottom we ran into a New Zealander whose boat was moored ahead of us; a fifty-foot Brixham trawler. From his masthead the only flag he flew was the skull and crossbones. He was only too pleased to show us where he did the bottom on his boat, and that afternoon at full tide took us across from the yacht club and around a sand-spit into a very small bay where we tied up fore-and-aft. Never have I seen such an agile man. Even before I had a chance, he had the anchor on his shoulder and jumped into the water, planting it firmly in the sand.

There were two others on his boat: a young Scottish chap and a woman around thirty-five, not counting a pint-sized monkey, six inches high, fully grown, that livened up the boat somewhat and had, as I found out, the habit of urinating on anyone who picked it up. 'Old Nick,' as he was called, had brought his boat out from England on his way to Australia first, and then Auckland, where he intended to fit the boat out for an around-the-world cruise. There was not much of 'Old Nick' when you looked at him, but for a man of seventy he wasn't doing too bad. He was almost ready to sail and his first stop from Panama was to be Samoa.

When the tide was dropping we went for a swim and got our first taste of the effect the Gulf Stream has in these parts. The shock of the cold water after the warm water on the other side of the canal was surprising, and I think it was even colder than Yarmouth in England. With the tide out we lay over on an angle of thirty degrees, and for the next two days had to get used to living this way while we painted the bottom and topsides. As this did not take long to do, Duff and I would spend most of the day, while we were waiting for the tide, along the beaches and among the rocks, picking up pieces of semi-precious stones such as jasper, milk opal and agate of many different colours, including some nice black. I found a crystal and held it up to get the full light on its faces, it was absolutely perfect. What laws of attraction and rejection were involved in its creation, what form of consciousness does it have to have, what are its limits of pressure and heat that bring it altogether?

As soon as we had finished the painting we took the boat back and moored off the yacht club. We spent three more days there painting the deck and booms and getting the boat ready. We had a few more stores to get and took on thirty gallons of petrol besides our cans and lashed our drum forward against the mast. This was to help us through the doldrums belt. Panama City was much the same as the other side of the canal. The area where the Americans had built stood out from the rest of the town which was fairly shabby in places and seemed to have more bars than anything else, but we really did not get much of a chance to look around.

The people ashore were very friendly and went out of their way to show us places we were looking for. The Americans who were policing here, as well as the other side of the canal, used to amuse us the way they walked down the street with their .45 revolvers strapped low on their hips, some of them giving a better performance than Rock Hudson in the Last Sunset, as they got along with their hands hovering over gun butts in cut-away holsters. The yacht club here was very helpful by allowing us to get paint and petrol through one of their members at a reduced price. The club itself was a big place with three storeys.

The anchorage was not the best as the tide was very strong and the ships passing all the time rolled us around a fair bit. Our dinghy went adrift but was luckily found and brought back by one of the members. The last night we went ashore to the club and had a beer. The television set there was popular and it was strange to see the line of big, burly men sitting, eyes glued to the screen as if they were mesmerised. Looking for a place to eat we ended up in the big dining-room and, before we could back out, were shown to a table. The menu, which was thrust into our hands, started off with pound steaks and got better and better as you went down. As we had only two dollars, I kept my eyes on the knives, forks and spoons that were laid out for six courses, ordered three hamburgers, and was glad to get out of there.

The next morning, which was Sunday the 25th of March, we slipped from the buoy at seven o'clock, and with a good tide behind us started out through the Gulf of Panama on the start of the second half of our trip with US$24.30 in the kitty and our whiskey. The wind was light all day and we sailed through many schools of porpoise. The wind fell off at sundown and, as the current was taking us towards the coast, we started the motor and used it all night, running through strange, white patches on the water that looked like milk.

Chapter Twelve

Panama to Galapagos – The Doldrums

There was no wind the next day and, after waiting until midday for it to come, we gave up and motored to a small island six miles away. There were porpoises everywhere in these waters. In the passage between the island and the mainland the bottom was red with snapper and the surface water churned with fish. Motoring around until we found a small bay we went in to anchor and ran aground on the coral, but with two of us up forward the motor pulled us off with no damage.

After we had anchored we put the dinghy over the side and went ashore. The only building on the island was a small, grass shack. The four men living there were stretched out in their hammocks and showed no sign of moving for anybody. There was a small coconut plantation as well as many fruit trees, and there was a well just behind the shack. Beside the door, laying in the shade, was the biggest sow I have ever seen. The only reason I knew it was still alive was that it got up periodically and walked down to the water's edge where it submerged itself in the salt water. Inside the shack, strips of dried fish hung from the rafters above an open fireplace. Other than the hammocks a small wooden table was the only thing in there. Bill was able to talk a little Spanish to them and before we went back to the boat we were given a stalk of bananas and a big papaw for which they refused to take any money.

There were thousands of seagulls on the island, but unfortunately no

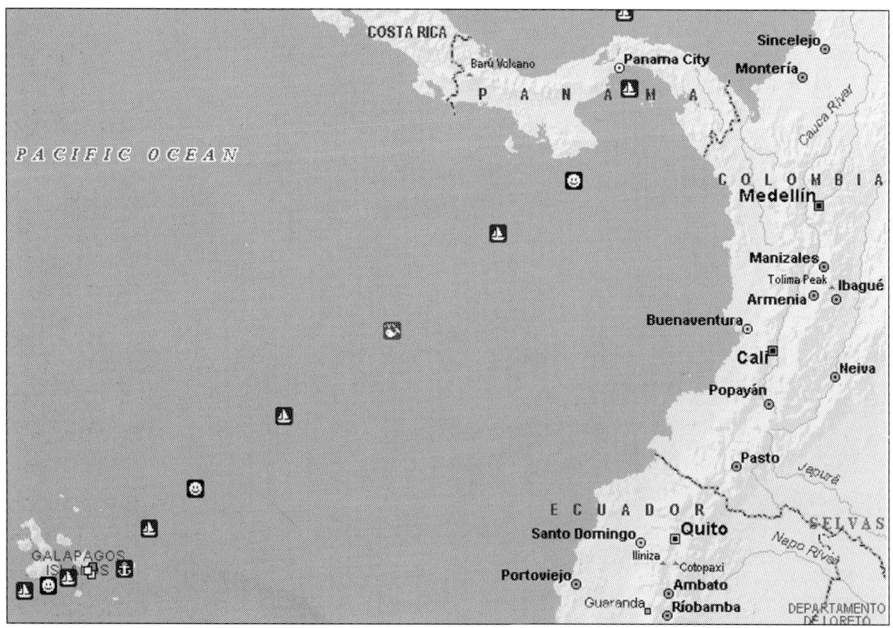

Panama to Galapagos.

eggs. Some of these birds were quite pretty and had a bright, red breast. Back on board while we got the fishing gear ready, Bill took some rum ashore and gave it to the men. Duff did not have much luck with his lines so we decided to try out our new face mask. I went below for a look around and down in this 'other world' there were fish by the hundreds, all different types and colours. Schools of fish passed under the boat, swimming around nigger-heads and passing through small valleys of coral. Never had I thought so many fish could be in one place. Unfortunately, I could not dive much deeper than fifteen feet because no matter what I did I could not clear my ears, so Bill went down with the speargun to get our tea.

I lost count of how many times he came up to reload the gun, spluttering as he tried to tell us the size of the fish and how the spear just would not go into them. After about an hour swimming around a lump of coral he came face to face with a ten-pound cod, which was just as surprised as Bill but whose reflexes were slower. Using the spear as a bayonet and pulling the trigger at the same time, he managed to get the spear in far enough but let the gun go as soon as the cod went under a rock, then came up, got a knife and went back and killed it.

It was a beautiful fish, and there were many more like it and much bigger. With a good speargun Bill could have filled our cockpit with fish in a few hours. That night at sundown, and up until we went to bed at ten o'clock, the bay was alive with life. Many sharks and swordfish cut the water as they hunted. Long, narrow barracuda shot across the water with their tails leaving a phosphorescence-trail as the hunter became the hunted. Sea-snakes swam past the boat with a smooth motion, and turtles thrust their snake-like heads out of the water, breathing with a loud gasp, then disappearing into the darker depth with a round, green glow. Down below in our bunks the crunching of the reef builders at work penetrated through the hull, reminding us that yet another form of marine life was busy at work. Through the hull also, at regular intervals, could be felt the vibrations of the shocks from a volcano that was erupting – and when we passed it it lit the sky with its flame and fire.

We sailed at seven in the morning and to our surprise sighted Cape Mala at eight. This was due to a strong south-west current pushing us all the way from Panama. After clearing the cape Bill and I sat down and started to work out our first longitude sight. Since he learnt his out of Hiscock's book and I out of Mary Blewitt's, there was a lot of arguing. I don't know how many sheets of paper we used but it was quite a bit, and after three hours of mental strain came up with an answer that put us seventeen miles off our position. We thought this was pretty good: at least our answer did not put us on top of a mountain range.

A strong wind came up at sundown but fell away during the night. The next day, using one of the spinnakers as a staysail, we hoisted the other one as a trysail instead of having our gaff and boom swinging and banging around. This sail cut down our rolling by 90%. We had two days of light winds and calms. During this time the sea life that passed us was fantastic. The sea was like a big aquarium in which we had a front seat. All types of jellyfish passed us, some with a small, white, round disc in the centre of them, others drifting past like leaves falling from a tree in autumn. One of the strangest was something like a sea-slug, brown in colour, four feet long and six inches thick.

Plenty of sea-snakes were in the water and turtles surfaced from time to time. Stingrays would fling themselves out of the water trying to free themselves of parasites, coming down on the surface with a resounding whack. Plenty of dorado were around and we caught two big ones, about fifty pounds each. We salted most of this down and fed quite a bit to a third fish which got so tame that it would take the pieces of fish six inches from our hands. He followed the boat for over a week. That is, I think it was the same fish, and he soon learnt to keep out of harpoon distance.

Two sharks followed us astern nearly all day before one came close enough to iron. The harpoon took it square in the centre of the head and, after giving it plenty of time to wear itself out, we pulled it alongside where Duff got stuck into it with the cutlass. While this bloody operation was in process the sucker-fish attached to it dropped off and went to look for another free ride. When its stomach was opened out dropped small sharks and, on hitting the water, began swimming away feebly, the umbilical cord still attached, trailing behind as they moved through the water. The shark was only five-foot long but we had to cut it in half to bring it on board. It had quite a few parasites on the top fins and, when we threw the tail back into the sea until it disappeared into the depths, the tail still went through the motions of swimming.

We were about to throw the gutted top half back in the water when Duff decided to keep its teeth. He was about to open its jaws with his hands when it was suggested to try with the cutlass first. No sooner was the blade in its mouth than the jaws opened and snapped shut and its evil eyes flickered its hate.

It was still calm in the morning. Just after we got up a log, much longer than our boat and about two-foot-six through, drifted around us for a while. Not long after that we began going through patches of current that disturbed the sea like a tide rip and could be heard a fair distance away. The wind came up again that night and we sailed along close-hauled, making good mileage. The next day we had squalls and late in the afternoon sighted Malpelo Island about twenty miles away. This island is only a mile long and eight-hundred-odd feet high. It looked as bare as if it had just been thrust up from the ocean floor and was waiting for the first coconut to drift ashore and take root, or a bird to land and leave seed. It showed us that our longitude sights were not too far out and except for one or two little things we found out later, we were correct. That night there were more squalls and in the morning we found that we had circled the island.

We had fickle winds for days, that kept us changing our rig, and a lot of squalls. It was during one of these that we lost Bill over the side. We were both up forward doing something to the headsails. The boat was pounding a bit and caught Bill off balance, flipping him neatly over the side in a backward somersault. As I was working ahead of him I did not see him go. The first I knew was when Duff at the helm made the understatement of the year by remarking casually, "Hello, Bill's gone!" When I looked around he was already half-way back onboard, spitting water, with a surprised look on his face like a person who does not know quite what happened.

The wind remained fickle for another three days: squalls, rain, thunder, lightning and overcast skies that made really miserable weather. Then the sun came out for the first time in six days and we were able to take a sight that put us thirty-seven miles north of the Equator. That night we used our motor on a flat, calm sea until dawn, and that day, since we would be crossing the Equator, we decided to have an Equatorial dinner. There was quite a bit of competitive spirit with the cooking since we had all started to take turns. Duff cooked some toffee which, of course, was gone before it had time to cool. Bill cooked dinner that night, three courses of it; mushroom soup, fish cakes and tinned fruit and custard.

Actually, we were running along the Equator but did not find out until eight the next day so I was caught for another dinner. We decided it was as good an excuse as any and I ventured to try my hand at some coconut cakes and jam rolls. I won't say they turned out exactly as they were supposed to, but at least I know now how a housewife feels after slaving over a hot stove for hours and all her labour disappears in five minutes. It took me four hours to cook these treats on our stove and I swear they were all gone before sixty seconds were up. There was no doubt that we were in the main Gulf Stream or Peruvian Current when we crossed the Equator as we were pushed ahead twenty and thirty miles a day by our sights.

The weather now more than made up for those six days of cloud and rain. It was like an autumn day back in the valley: the sky and horizon crystal clear, the water much too cold to swim in. The evenings and mornings had a touch of winter in them, like the wind coming down off the mountains warning you that the first snow was not far away. The nights were quite cold and all our coats and jumpers were pulled out of the lockers again. If anyone had told me I would be sitting on the Equator wrapped up in a sheepskin coat, I don't think I would have believed them.

The nights were as good as the days, the clear sky filled with a million stars, and I enjoyed sitting at the helm watching them appear in the sky as if they were old friends. Their names I would never know, but where they pointed to on the compass was fixed in my mind so that going on watch I looked for them instinctively. It was one such of these nights that I watched a meteorite, surrounded by a bluish flame, arch into the sea about twenty miles away. I was not sure, it could have been my imagination, but I thought that I heard a hiss or a splash as it disappeared into the water.

On Sunday the 8th of April we took another sight that put us on latitude 0° and longitude 87° 33'. That meant we should sight the islands next day. We had used our motor all night on a calm sea and were moving along under sail with a light wind. There were quite a lot of patches of current on the sea and sometimes we came across places where the currents seemed to meet. Here, where the colder Peruvian Current met the warmer water of the Pacific, was a long, whitish, yellow stripe winding its way across the ocean in a rough line, stretching away as far as the eye could see. When we sailed our boat over this line, and had a closer look, the line itself did not vary in width but remained three-to-four inches wide. It was probably due to some very small sea life killed by the change of temperature in the water.

We had seen quite a few rays in the water during the day and as the sun started to get low in the sky I went below to get tea, while Duff stayed at the helm. It was close to sundown when he gave a yell and made the statement that he had just seen a splash of water go sixty feet up in the air. To this I made a reply of one word, "Balls!", and went on getting tea, but when he made it again I thought I had better see if he was suffering hallucinations and went up to have a look around. He had not seen anything make the splash and as I stood there I saw one of the most unforgettable sights I have ever seen. A whale, about eighty feet long, hurled itself from the sea before it dropped back again.

We saw the pod of whales then and, as they blew, smoke-like vapour rose up from the sea. This one big whale kept breaching, turning in the water until his forked tail was arched against the skyline, then diving deep he would come hurling up from the depths, breaking through the water with his massive head that sent spray and foam in all directions. He would fling himself clear of the water, hang motionless in the air for a few seconds, with his awe-inspiring bulk outlined against the sun, then drop with a terrific splash that sent water into the air, just as Duff said, around sixty feet.

There was no wind again that night, and we ran our motor for fourteen hours. In the morning the sea was like glass, the sky was overcast as usual until around nine, then it cleared into a beautiful, warm day. Our noon sight put us twenty-six miles off the island of San Cristobal, and when it had not appeared by late afternoon we started to look for some fault in our sights. It was a bit of a let down because we thought we had the workings of the sights correct. Bill was down at the chart with a heavy frown on his face. I was on the bowsprit refusing to move, although the sun already had gone, when I saw it, just the tip of a mountain. Then it was gone.

By our dead-reckoning, we were only sixteen miles off the island. The visibility was good that day for at least thirty miles, so we thought, but we were to find out a lot of things before we left those islands. The wind dropped soon after dark and we started our motor again. I had the first watch and after motoring for three hours ran into heavy, thick fog, a real pea-souper. The fog was so thick that I could barely make out the bow of our boat and the condensation was running down my face. Suddenly, quite clearly and precisely, I heard a voice telling me to "switch the motor off". I thought that I was hallucinating but got up and went forward to the bow – nothing. I had hardly sat down in the cockpit when the voice told me again "switch the motor off". I went forward, concerned, using all my senses, seeing, hearing, smelling – nothing. Back in the cockpit again I had a third warning. The voice said "this is your last warning – switch the motor off". I pulled the throttle lever up and as the sound of the motor died, from straight ahead came the sound of breakers filling the night. I called out to Bill and Duff and swung the boat to port – breakers. I turned to starboard – breakers. I then did the only thing I could do, reverse back out to sea. There was nothing to see, only the sound. How far off they were would only be guessing.

It may have been better had we hove to for the rest of the night but instead we ran out to sea for five miles, then took a parallel course to clear the island for another five miles, then turned to run down the island. In the morning the fog was just as thick and there was no sign of land nor a sound to be heard on a dead flat sea. I had plenty of time to think of the night before.

I had read, and been told of, strange things happening at sea. It is not surprising when you realise that we are in the same environment as the mystics, monks, priests and nuns who go into retreat far away from civilization and its distractions. We, too, spend time in total solitude when alone in the cockpit for hours on end, for days, weeks, and longer. The mind quietens down to its natural state and the mundane thoughts stop. Duff and I had already compared what was happening to us during these long hours of silence. We agreed that we were both looking at the not-so-nice things we had done in our lives. Steering by the stars for hours on end is a form of Tibetan meditation, as is focusing on a compass. The silent mind concentrating on a single object allows the inner self access to the outer self and those powers within to develop. Most sailors would laugh at this, but then they have not heard the voice or the breakers. I know that my dimensional world will never be quite the same again. I also know that I will investigate these uncharted waters one day.

We hove-to and waited for the sun to come out and the fog to clear. We waited for hours, sitting in the cockpit, not very happy with the situation. I don't know who was the most surprised out of the three of us when a head suddenly popped out of the sea in front of us and we looked into the soft, brown eyes of our first seal. He was very curious and came half out of the water trying to peer over the side of the boat. He swam around for quite a while before he went away leaving us in a good mood. At eleven-thirty the fog started to lift and when it cleared there was the island two miles away with breakers washing up on a long, white beach. The only trouble was we were on the wrong side of the island. How we got there I do not know, and how close we were to the shore, and the small patches of rock that stood out of the sea at the top of the island, we will never know – it was bad enough going through there in daylight and we motored around and down the other coast. As there was no chance of reaching Wreck Bay before dark we dropped anchor in a little cove, using the leadline as we went in. We sighted the island fourteen days out from Panama, but as we used our motor it would be hard to say just how long it would take under sail alone.

Chapter Thirteen

Galapagos Islands

We went ashore for a look around, although there was little to see where we had landed. The bush was not very tall and mostly dry, but very thick in places. Bill went diving for crayfish and caught a big one for tea. Duff spent most of his time chasing bright-red crabs around the rocks for fish bait. Back on board he caught some nice cod and bream for breakfast. After tea we sat on deck and watched the changing colours play across this strange scenery. From the sea at first it looked like open plain country, but closer it turned out to be bush, with rugged hills and mountains of different-coloured rock, some patches of hills standing alone, looking out of place among the flat land.

There was a good offshore breeze all night and we got underway early in the morning to arrive in Wreck Bay between eight and four, so we would miss the $10 fine we heard they liked to charge yachts stopping there. It was a fine sail down the coast with beautiful weather, and turtles and seals keeping us company most of the way. We passed close to Kicker Rock. This rock is a good landmark and rises almost vertical from depths of fifty fathoms to stand four-hundred-and-eighty-six-feet high, and looks like a square tower. We were so busy taking the boat around a shoal and getting our sails down that we were abeam of the little town before we noticed it, so we motored in and anchored off the jetty.

These islands are controlled by the Ecuadorian Navy and in no time

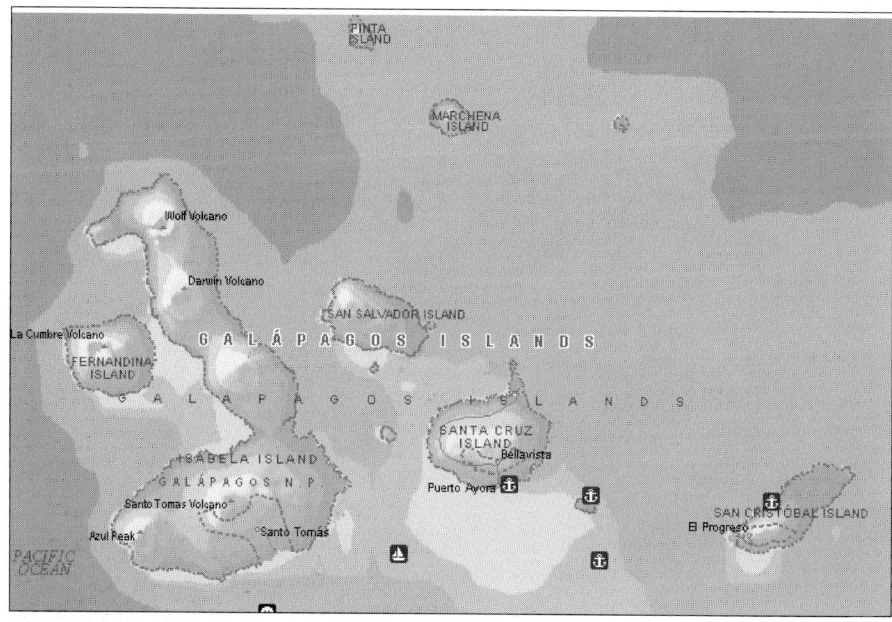

Galapagos Islands.

we had some of them eyeing us from the jetty. They came aboard from a landing barge that would have comfortably held around a hundred men. There were four officers, all immaculately dressed, one doctor and a petty officer. Somehow all of them managed to fit down below and check our papers thoroughly. They were quite friendly and asked a few questions. We were so pleased when they did not mention a fine that we broke open a bottle of rum, and I guess I was a little heavy handed when I poured. The PO knocked his drink back without blinking an eye. The doctor's hand fairly shook as he put his away, and it left most of the officers speechless. I was watching one whose eyes started to bulge after the first sip, and by the time he had finished the shot I thought they were going to pop. He looked around at me as if I had given him poison and managed to gasp one word, "Gasolenea!" They left quite hurriedly after that, before we could offer them another drink, and told Bill to go to the Navy office in the morning to get his clearance.

We went ashore in the afternoon to have a look around the town. It did not take long as the place was not very big. It reminded me of a typical western Queensland town back in Australia; the same dry heat and dirt roads pounded into fine dust that swirled into the air with the faintest breeze. Many of the stores had old, wooden, floor walks in front of them. All that was missing was the bat-winged doors. Instead of goats along the main street, as you would find in Queensland, here it was donkeys that you had to walk around. Even the town's water supply was the same; a big turkey-nest dam. I cannot say that I liked San Cristobal, mainly because of how the people lived. Many of the old gold miners' shacks back in the hills of New Zealand are better than some of the houses lived in here. The naval establishment was quite an impressive building built of solid stone. As usual, the big church stood out like a palace compared with the rest of the place.

Many of the people lived back in the hills on small farms. The patches of cleared land could be seen from the shore but were much too far away for us to walk. We did however, manage to see a Galapago, or giant tortoise, after which this group of islands was named. He looked decidedly unhappy sitting in a fowl-house with only hens for company. I think I am right in saying these islands are the only place left where these big land tortoises are found. The whalers in olden days killed them off by the hundreds for their meat, and they can grow up to a ton in weight.

In the morning we decided to sail as soon as we got our clearance. Bill went ashore to the Navy office, only to come back to say they wanted $10 as we had come into harbour during their siesta time. He told them that we had hove-to all night so we would come in during the proper hours and argued that we arrived before the siesta hours, which we did by our watch but their time was an hour ahead. He also told them that we only had $15. Of course, like most of the people we met on our trip, they assumed that because we were on a yacht we must also have a lot of money, thought the $15 was a very big joke.

I didn't think we had any chance of getting out of paying, so I loaded an old sock with $10 in nickels, dimes and cents and Bill and I went over to have another try. We argued for over half an hour, or rather, I should say, I did. Bill did not get a chance to get a word in edgeways, and neither did the PO. I did very well seeing I could only speak six words of Spanish. At least I made a lot of noise. To the PO, the law was the law. To me, $15 was $15, and he was not going to get any part of it if I could help it. In the end his resistance broke down and he did what I wanted. He took us to an officer who said he would take the matter up with the Port Captain. They looked at me with distaste and told Bill that only he was to come back and find out the answer at three o'clock. The answer was that we would pay no fine, but the trouble we had to go to would not be worth it to anyone who had the money.

We took the boat alongside the jetty for water. The pilot book described the jetty as being somewhat dilapidated in 1935. It certainly had not improved since then. I think the barnacles had done a fine job holding it up for so long. It turned out to be quite a job to take on the water. There was a big swell running that broke our lines like cotton. I must admit our lines were getting a little ripe by this time. It was probably just as well. I hate to think of the fine they would have thought up if we pulled part of the jetty down. It was about half an hour before we had topped our tanks up. This was accomplished mainly by brute strength. While Bill and I held up the boat, Duff wrestled with a six-inch wire-bound hose that was so heavy it almost broke his back trying to lift it. The water was half and half; half sand and half water which was filled with all sorts of wogs and beasties so that we had to strain and boil every drop we used.

Just as we were starting to motor out of the harbour we were told there were still more papers to pick up ashore. As the dinghy was on board, Bill swam ashore, ran along the beach like a madman, marched into the Navy office and stood dripping water all over the floor while the papers were being signed. He reappeared running back along the beach with the papers held high in his hand like a torchbearer in the Olympic Games. He hailed a boat from the jetty that brought him out to where I was laying-to. No sooner was he on board than the sails were up and we were on our way, leaving quite a few people staring after us, convinced that we were all a little crazy.

As it was four o'clock when we sailed we were not far from the island at sundown. As the sun disappeared so did the wind, and not long after that a heavy fog rolled in. There was a very light wind all night and dawn found us off an island, but it was off our port instead of starboard. Duff was still at the helm and the boat was dead on our course for the island of Santa Cruz. It was my turn to cook breakfast and, during that time and until breakfast was over, the boat was bedlam as the three of us argued as to what island it was, just where we were, and how we got there. Bill argued that it was still blue same island we had left, I said it was an island off Santa Cruz, and Duff had us even further north.

As we motored in towards the island we could not pick out any landmarks that we knew, and none that covered any of the northern islands. The chart showed a west-north-west current from San Cristobal at one-and-a-half to two knots. As we neared shore we headed for a small bay, and as we got closer two goats stepped out of the bush and walked along the sandy beach. No-one bothered about where we were after that. There was only one thought – fresh meat. The boat was anchored in record time and the dinghy put over the side. Two hundred yards away on a patch of rocks a colony of seals barked their protest at our invasion of their privacy. Bill decided to swim ashore with flippers and goggles on and see if he could spot any crayfish.

Duff and I loaded the dinghy up with enough weapons to take on the Ecuadorian Navy and shoved off for the shore. So intent were we on the tracks of the goats on the beach, that we almost stepped out of the dinghy onto the back of a four-foot ray that had enough sense to get out of our way. We then unloaded the weapons, the harpoon tied onto the flagstaff, two knives, a small axe and a cutlass. No sooner had we finished this when a five-foot shark came swimming along only four feet from the edge of the water, with his belly a few inches off the bottom, while Bill swam straight towards it.

It took a lot of yelling before he even looked up and then, while I kept my eyes on the shark, Duff went through the pantomime of someone getting his leg forcibly removed. It seemed a very long while before the message penetrated but, when it did, he moved. I think he was still swimming when he was a good way up on the beach. The goat hunt turned out to be a flop. Our yelling would have frightened away anything within a two-mile radius and sitting on the beach, talking about meat, our eyes kept going back to the seals. Someone remarked, "Whalers used to eat seals." There were two "yeahs" and the hunt was on. I threw the harpoon at one and hit it just right, but instead of dropping it took off like a rocket leaving the flagstaff behind.

That was the last time I saw the harpoon, but not the seal. Out of the belly of one of six small sharks Duff caught that night were lumps of fresh seal meat. We finished up wading out to the colony on the rocks, and I managed to hit a small one over the head with the flagstaff. He was lying in shallow water enjoying the sunshine and I felt like a murderer as I carried him back, but meat is meat and in no time Duff had him on a flat rock and the knife flashing red in the sunlight. We got quite a few pounds of good meat from him and took the fat back on board to render down for cooking oil.

We took a sight while we were on board and at first could not believe it, but there was no mistake. We were south instead of north on the island of Espanola, the southernmost island of the group. The current had taken us forty-six miles south in twelve hours. In the afternoon, Duff and I went ashore to have a look for some more goats and must have walked about six miles through thick, short scrub and over ridges of very rough, volcanic rock. In some places there were small, open, red-soil plains. Most of the trees growing on these plains were tall cactus. It was dry, stony, desert country, with no sign of water anywhere, and the bones of the goats told their own story. The only live one we saw was in thick scrub and we had no chance to get near him.

We did not come back empty-handed. On a promontory, jutting out a thousand feet above the sea, we came across a flock of quail. Duff must have had more practice breaking windows when he was going to school than I did because he managed to get three with almost as many stones, while I got one. It was a shame to kill them as they had no fear of men whatsoever. Like some New Zealand birds they spent more time on the ground than they did in the air, and after this lot we would not kill any more while we were in the islands. It gave us more pleasure to have them swinging on a branch over our shoulder or hopping around at our feet, looking up at us curiously, head cocked to one side as if they were saying, "What are these strange animals? I haven't seen them before."

What a meal we had that night: seal steaks, quail cooked in the pressure-cooker, and, to top it off, a big crayfish that Bill had caught while we were away. That night Duff caught half a bucket of bream in about an hour, as well as the sharks, so breakfast and dinner were looked after. We decided to sail as soon as there was enough wind for us to combat the current, and at midnight the sky cleared and we got underway and set our course for the island of Santa Maria, around forty miles west of us, on roughly the same latitude. Just as we started to clear Espanola, the wind dropped and the fog rolled in.

We started the motor to run clear of the island and it was not until dawn that a light wind came up and we turned the motor off. We had kept it running so we would not be pushed south – clear of the islands altogether. It was cloudy all day and we were not able to get a sight. There was no sign of land and it was not until late in the day that we sighted an island off our starboard bow and started our motor to get there before dark.

As we got closer we could see the island was much too small for Santa Maria and its steep, rugged cliffs did not hold much promise of us finding a bay to anchor in for the night. I hated the thought of what the current and fog would do to us if we had to lay-off all night, and as we motored up the length of the island we sighted another one to the north-west. It appeared to be a big island about ten miles off which we took to be Santa Cruz. That meant the current had pushed us north this time; twenty-two miles in eighteen hours, and that the island we were circling was Santa Fe. There was only one anchorage on the island and, of course, it had to be on the other side. With our motor going full bore we raced against the darkness that would come with the going of the sun, which was disappearing much too fast from the sky.

For an island only four miles long and two-and-a-half miles wide, it seemed a very long time before we saw the little bay ahead of us, but what a bay it was. Actually, it was an inlet about half a mile long with a natural breakwater, and going through the narrow opening we caught a glimpse of nature with all its beauty and life. The island was covered with cactus – not just cactus as I had seen before, small and insignificant, but tall trees of it with trunks a foot and more through, with lofty branches covered in pear that reached out and up towards the sky. On our left, on top of the cliff, a mob of different-coloured goats browsed along close to the edge. On the right, along the breakwater, seals stood up to bark and stare, their skins glistening as they reflected the changing light.

Ahead of us were two small beaches, packed with seals adding their chorus of barks to those on the rocks; some of them weaving down over the white sand and into the water to swim out, diving and playing around the boat. The bottom was clear, white sand with a depth of no more than twelve feet and it was alive with life. Dozens of turtles, many of them over four feet long, broke water around us to look, gasp a breath, and disappear with a flurry of flippers, leaving a trail of bubbles behind them. Scores of black rays swam through the water with their bird-like motion, the tips of their flaps cutting through the water looking like shark fins. So thick were these rays, and some of them so big, over ten feet wide, that we thought they were patches of rock on the bottom. After we had anchored there was just enough light left to row ashore and have a closer look at this island, so full of life and animals, and the only men there to spoil it were us.

The next morning Duff was up early and caught three fish for breakfast. The two of us then went ashore to see if we could find any goats. We had made a rough spear out of the flagstaff and an old screwdriver but returned empty-handed without sighting anything. Back on board we watched with hungry eyes turtles swimming by and it did not take us long to work out a plan to catch one. Bill had noticed a few sleeping on the bottom while he was spear-fishing so, with me in the dinghy, he swam ahead with the harpoon line in his hand, a wire noose on the end of it, until he saw unsuspecting turtles enjoying a sleep on the bottom, then down he would dive and sneak up behind them. The first two took off like a rocket, but he managed to put the noose clean over the head of a third one.

The next thing I knew he was yelling at me to keep the line tight, but there was no need to worry about that. He had put the wire over a turtle around four feet long and weighing over a hundred pounds. While I tried to keep my balance, haul in the slack line, and get the dinghy ashore, the turtle found out that it was not a dream after all and was towing me around in circles. We managed to get ashore with Bill swimming, half-towing the dinghy and the turtle. A trip back to the boat brought Duff with the buckets and knives and in no time he was standing with one foot in the shell, cutting off big chunks of quivering red meat. No sooner was the job finished than we were on board cooking our first meal of turtle meat. I have always been a beef eater, but I would change to turtle meat any day. So delicious was the meat and so hungry were we for it, that we behaved like three savages and gorged ourselves, until by dinner time the next day there was not a bit left. The following day, late in the afternoon, we caught a smaller one – but this did not taste as good. We found out later that the smaller turtles are fish eaters and not as appetizing, while the bigger ones feed on seaweed.

The next day was fine and sunny and, although there seemed to be good visibility, we could not see the island of Santa Cruz and I doubt if we could see any more than six miles. The days were hot, so hot in fact that, even as brown as we were, the sun still burnt us. At night it was cool, so cool we needed our blankets.

The water was very cold and after fifteen minutes in it your teeth would start to chatter. This did not stop Bill though. He spent a lot of time in the water and whenever we wanted a fish he would take the spear, swim over to a small patch of coral and always come back with a three- or four-pounder. He was inclined to get too absorbed in what he was doing and would forget about the sharks that sometimes came in hunting for food.

The seals did not bother us much in the water. Sometimes they would swim around us curiously. Usually they gave us quite a start when we first saw their shape through the face mask as we would take them for sharks.

Duff and I frightened six months growth out of Bill, as he was spear-fishing under a wall, by putting a big bull seal into the water a foot in front of him. As the seal hit the water, angry at being disturbed, it turned and charged up and down in front of Bill who had his back to the wall using his small spear as a sword. It was only later that we found out how dangerous these animals can be, and both Duff and I found out what it was like to have a big bull seal charging around us in the water. I don't mind admitting that I somehow managed to climb into the dinghy backwards, after swallowing a snorkel of water, when I first saw the shape of the seal fill my mask.

On shore these bull seals were not to be trifled with, as we found out when we threw a stick at a big one asleep on the sand. It was three very surprised blokes who jumped back about six feet as he got up, roared and charged through us to the water.

Duff was the only one who was caught in the water with a shark. He was diving around a patch of coral when a five-foot shark circled him a few times. Luckily, he did not see it himself and swam unconcerned back to the boat. His face was something to see when we pointed the shark out to him.

After three days on the island we sailed early in the morning for Santa Cruz. The wind was fickle all day, and crossing between the islands we had three different sets of currents. It was getting late in the day when we were entering the bay and we used our motor, keeping close to the high cliff that showed eighteen fathoms on the chart. We were looking to steer for a small white beach that was given in the pilot book. We found out later that had it not been high tide when we went in, we would have ended up on some rocks under the cliff that were not marked. As for the beach, it had disappeared some years before. Not knowing just where to go we headed for some fishing-boats anchored close to a low cliff. They turned out to belong to the Augermyer brothers, and a deep voice boomed out across the water telling us where to anchor.

The Naval Port Captain came on board and looked at our papers. We had thought we would be free of fines when we left San Cristobal, but this fine system carries on through most of the islands. We were lucky to arrive just before the deadline at six o'clock but if we wanted to sail outside of office hours – that is before eight in the morning and after six at night – there was another fine of $10, even though the papers were made out in working hours.

I liked Academy Bay. It was much different from San Cristobal with

House, Santa Cruz.

the settlement well laid out and clean. As in most places the buildings followed the bay around. The background of dry, stony ground gave way to high hill country. The green foliage there gave promise of lush growth. Here were the farms of the settlement, some of them belonging to Europeans of all nations who had settled here. Most of the people were Ecuadorian and generally lived in wooden houses. Quite a lot of new brick houses were being built in the town by an American who had been there around fifteen years. A line of tall palm trees planted by some thoughtful person years ago are the only ones in these islands and help break up the barren shore-line.

Close by our boat, along a low cliff, was a smaller settlement of a group of houses. These differed from all the others as they were built out of rough, basalt rock that lay around in uncountable tons. These rough stone houses built close to the edge of the cliff, with tall cactus around them, had a setting all of their own and belonged to the Augermyer brothers, their family and a few friends. These brothers were some of the first settlers in the islands. They left Germany around thirty years before and landed in Santa Cruz with a dream, a few tools and some seed for their first crop. Because they were not afraid to tackle anything, they are still there.

We did not meet one of the brothers who was away. We saw very little of Carl as he was busy taking scientists, studying wildlife, around the different islands, but we spent many interesting hours with Gus, talking about life and learning about these islands. There was nothing he liked better than to throw the clock away and sit down and yarn. He came on board the first night to see if there was anything we needed. He was a stocky man, genuine and frankly spoken, with strong principles. Life was a serious thing to him and yet a joke was a must. His dreams were still as strong as when he first landed on those shores.

He took us to one of the stone houses to meet an American family, who had sent one of their children along inviting us to come up for coffee. They were a friendly couple and made us feel at home. I lost count of the number of people who dropped in for a talk that night, and the little house was crowded as we swapped yarns about our trip and they told us about the boats pulling in there. All of them looked healthy and much younger than their years. The wonderful climate in these islands would have something to do with it, also their simple life that was not without its hardships.

The small stone house was comfortable and homely inside, even with its rough appearance. Bamboo rafters held up the iron roof and screen wire covered the big open windows. An open fireplace was in the centre of the room, and this was needed all winter even though the islands are almost on the Equator. The furniture was simple and much the same as some that our grandmothers used. As there was no electricity, oil-lamps gave an atmosphere almost forgotten in our modern age. All the cooking was done on kerosene stoves. The bread was home-made and how they turned out cakes and biscuits in some of their ovens was almost as amazing as the ovens themselves. Just about everything on the island had to be made out of what could be found there. This American woman proudly showed us the oven she had made from a four-gallon kerosene tin and, as for her bread and cakes, we had tasted none better.

When we returned on board that night, as tired as we were, there was no sleep for us. Mosquitoes bombarded us all night, and we must have looked a sorry sight in the morning because Gus took one look at us as he rowed past and arrived back with some repellent which he handed to us with a grin. It was a lifesaver as there was none to be bought on the island and after that we were able to sleep alright. We spent most of our time fishing and salting-down fish for the trip to the Marquesas. While Duff and I fished from the dinghy Bill spear-fished around the reef close by, something I would not like to have done, as the water was much too cold and he would come out almost blue, with scratches and cuts all over him from being thrown on the reef by the waves. Also, the sharks here were very bad. There were dozens and dozens of them.

Slowly we built up our supply of fish, salted and dried it on deck in the sun or hung it from the rigging, so that the boat looked like a Chinese fish-market and smelt just as bad. Duff would go out fishing every night for a couple of hours and always caught a few sharks. We had one for breakfast every day whilst we were there and found them no different from any other fish except that they were sweeter. Bill looked after dinner by bringing back crayfish when he found them. The American took him around to a bay along the coast where they dived for five hours in murky water, collecting twenty crays. We had three and the rest were divided among the people living close to our boat.

The sharing of food, such as fish, turtles and goats, was a common practice, and it was good to see people living together and going out of their way to help each other. While we were there they would send their healthy, brown-skinned children down to the boat with goat meat. The children would bring not only meat but cakes, biscuits, bread and sometimes home-made butter. All these things took a long time to make and flour and sugar were fairly expensive. Sometimes it was hard to find out just who made them and sent them down. The children usually stopped at the boat only long enough to say, "Mum sent this." Our usual reply was "Who do you belong to?", and they would give us some vague answer, point in a direction that covered half the island, and be away, rowing across the bay to get their cans full of brackish water that everyone drank. It was quite a row across the bay to get water as Bill found out when he topped up our tank, but those pint-sized kids managed without any trouble, rowing dinghies many times bigger than themselves.

I don't know how many children lived in the houses near our boat. I tried counting them once but gave up as I could not tell when they were doubling back. There seemed to be a continuous stream passing along the top of the cliff, walking or running over the sharp, basalt rock with the immunity that only children have. They always seemed to be busy doing something. All the washing-up was done by them, a chore they seemed to enjoy as it was done in the sea at the edge of the cliff, and usually ended up in a free-for-all in the water.

Gus's children were fairly old. His eldest son, John, was busy building his own boat as his father had done but, at eighteen, dissatisfied with life on the island, he was leaving in a short while to have a look at America and all its wonders. The second eldest, Pepe, did all the cooking and could beat a lot of women I know hands down.

I gave Gus a hand to carry some stones for the new house he was building. I am afraid we did not carry many as we spent more time talking and he invited the three of us to come for lunch. I did not know he had planned it all beforehand and what a lunch it was: turtle steak done in breadcrumbs and rice. It was on a dish so big that Pepe could hardly carry it and, after urging us to eat all we could, he then brought out a big bowl of blancmange pudding, making sure we had two helpings. Just as we were on bursting-point, he suggested we have a piece of cake to finish off the meal. I have seen plenty of cakes, but never one as big as this, an angel cake. He took it straight out of the kerosene refrigerator, and with a twinkle in his eye he cut off a slice each so big that I could not even get my hand around it. I don't think I have ever tasted anything so good, and the fact it was made by a thirteen-year-old boy was hard to believe. Gus was still not finished with us. Coffee came next, and I can safely say it was the best meal I had eaten for many years.

That night Gus took me on a turtle hunt. We set out not long after sundown in his longboat. I rowed while from the bows he guided me through a narrow passage into a big lagoon, thick with mangroves around the edge. I kept rowing while he stood at the bow with a gaff hook on a long pole, giving me directions as we moved around the quiet water. The only sounds were the oars as they scraped on the rowloccks and the plop of some fish as they hit the water. There was no sign of any turtles for the first hour, then the moon came out big and full, and with it came the turtles. We saw the first one close to the bottom of a high cliff and as he shot out into the open water, just a green glow, we took off after him with Gus guiding me right or left, as he hunched over the bow with the gaff, ready to strike. He then reached down and I would feel a shock go through the boat as the gaff struck home. The pole would come loose and I would take it as Gus braced himself against the pull of the turtle, slowly pulling it into the boat. I thought the first one was a monster, but Gus only laughed and said it was a baby compared to some. It took a fair bit of work getting it into the boat and lashing it down. There seemed to be turtles everywhere after that. Many times we chased and lost them. Sometimes they would turn out to be rocks on the bottom. We finished up with three big ones. The smaller ones we let go as soon as we caught them. With these three on board there was no room for any more.

The sharks started to come in as we left; dozens of them, cutting through the shallow water around the boat. It was a long row back, but I did not mind. Gus and I had plenty to talk about. The moon was still high in the sky and time did not matter: it was as if it stood still that night. The next day we were kept busy cutting up the meat and salting it. As the salt we had was fairly fine we swapped it for the coarse salt that had been dug out of the salt pans, or salt mine as they called it. When Duff and I had finished the salting, we took most of the meat back and put it on deck to dry in the sun. We had roughly a hundred pounds of it.

That night we went up to Gus's place and he showed us his treasures as he called them. He had collected them around the small bays on the odd times he was exploring the different islands, or when he had a few hours off from fishing. They were pieces of old china, earthenware jars, hand-blown bottles and parts of a rusted old cutlass. To many people they would just be a pile of junk, but to him each one was a treasure. In its own right, each piece had a story for him to track down. Pre-Inca remains have been found on the islands. Pirates not only frequented these waters but also had their farms ashore for food. After them came the whalers, all of them leaving their mark.

It was all these marks that Gus had looked for over the years and was still looking for. To him, all that glitters is not gold, and all treasure need not be silver or gold. He had his own name for this hobby of his and called it 'Stampiering'. To him it meant when you stop work and roll up the fishing lines, put your knife away and forget that you have any cares and worries, and forget that you are over fifty. There are places to explore, old campsites to hunt through and, if the day is warm and sunny, sit on a smooth rock that was placed there dozens of years before, and let your mind go back into those days of long ago. Perhaps you will be contented, and the piece of china in your hand will mean a little more than just a broken dish. Looking at Gus, and knowing him a little, as I did, I do not think that it would be such a bad thing if more people went 'Stampiering' a little.

The next day the three of us left the boat to walk up in the mountains. The only New Zealander on the island had a farm up there. We had met him and his Ecuadorian wife at Gus's place one night. His wife was a very pleasant woman and he was a typical Kiwi who went by the name of Sandy. He arrived on the island around ten years before, liked the place and stayed. The track we followed ran alongside a road they were trying to build from the coast to the farms. Like the road, the track was very rough and with our bare feet it was hard going. For the first few miles the country was dry and stony and the track wound slowly upwards.

It was hot, as hot as you would find in the desert of South Australia. The bush was stunted and dry, and in many places dying through lack of moisture. We passed quite a few natives bringing down their barrels and jars loaded onto donkeys to get the brackish water from the wells close to the sea. The country changed rather abruptly. The stones disappeared and the brownish soil was replaced by black, but it, too, was cracked and rubbly. Then the first green leaves and grass started to show and as we turned a bend in the track, we saw the first trees of any size: a clump of very tall balsa trees.

We were on the edge of the village before we realised it. Flowers grew everywhere and the houses, though small, were neat. Crossing over what was a playing field we entered another land: a jungle with tall trees, green and thick foliage that the sun could only penetrate with shafts of light that lit up the rich, moist, black soil underfoot. It was cool here and the moisture lay like drops of silver on the broad leaves. Not all was rosy in this garden, as Bill found out when he sat on a log covered in tiny fire ants.

After Bill had performed the best haka I had seen for quite a while as he tried to get the ants off, we carried on up the track, passing small farms. Some were no more than clearings in the bush and most of them ran a few head of stock. These were prime stock and in very good condition. Hundreds of wild cattle lived on these highlands but they were all claimed by the Navy. With the maze of tracks cutting through the bush we were soon lost, and went into a farm for directions. It turned out to belong to a seventy-year-old Norwegian who had lived there for thirty years. He took us along the track with the steps of a young man, even though his snow white beard almost reached his waist. There was no mistaking Sandy's place when we reached it. The Taranaki gates were a dead giveaway.

The track was through fairly flat land with good grass on which a few horses were grazing. Clumps of tall bamboo, useful for building, dominated the rows of orange trees, and these led up to his well-built stockyards. We met him here bringing in some more horses, riding loosely in the wooden saddle they all use. His house was old, surrounded by a hedge of colourful hibiscus. Fowls ran more or less wild among the abundant papaw trees and pineapples. We could only stop a few hours with Sandy because of the trip back. Adrian Hayter, he told us, spent a night there on his way through to New Zealand.

His farm was not very big but had almost everything that a man needs to live. We took a walk over the rich soil that would grow anything. Sandy told us it was the driest year he had known, with no rain for ten months. Still it was not dry, as being high up in the land it got a lot of moisture from the atmosphere. Coffee and cocoa beans grew wild. There were grapefruit trees with plenty of fruit and the lower fruit eaten off by the cattle he ran. There were not many, but they, too, were in good condition and were currently grazing in the banana crop. The orange trees had plenty of fruit on them, but Sandy told us that with rain the fruit grows twice as big and the limbs break under the weight of the loaded trees.

The grass was small and stunted, but in a good year it grows up higher than a man on horseback and the track we came up has two feet of mud on it. Every type of vegetable will grow here but, like the fruit, there is hardly any market for it. Everything has to be packed down on donkeys and the price so small that it is hardly worthwhile, so the fowls, pigs and the rest of the stock eat most of the fruit, and what falls on the ground goes back into the soil. This is not such a waste as in our cities where tons of foodstuffs are destroyed just to keep the prices up.

Before we left, Sandy gave us a small gift to take back to his mother in Christchurch as well as loading us up with some grapefruit, oranges and a few pineapples. We took what was called the old track back down to the coast. It was well worn and a lot easier walking. We met quite a few girls bringing back water, walking alongside their laden donkeys. They had flashing smiles, jet-black eyes and coppery skin and, as tired as he was, Duff would have needed very little urging to start back up the track after them. It was dark when we got back to the boat and I didn't realise I had so many muscles that could ache. Next morning the three of us got out of our bunks like old men of ninety, Bill especially. He had to be straightened up forcibly.

The supplies Gus had ordered for us came down from the hill in the afternoon; four bunches of bananas, a dozen big squash and one-hundred-and-fifty pound of potatoes, then we got a little sugar and rice and topped up all our water tins. As we were going back to the island of Santa Fe for a day or two, we filled up everything on board that would hold water. That night we went up to say good-bye to the Americans, and before we left Mrs McGough gave us some of the card paintings she did in her spare time.

Gus told us that this family was the only one out of a hundred families who came out from America to settle in the islands that persevered and stayed. Perhaps the other ninety-nine expected too much. Those who came looking for a place to make money would have been sadly disappointed. Quite a number would have been taken in by the writers of today who no longer write facts, but who write for the big dream industry that we need. A lot would have liked to escape the tempo of our times and get away from a civilisation that threatens to destroy itself with nuclear weapons, but they lack the spirit of their forefathers. The rocks are there, if they feel like spitting on their hands and start building. The earth is waiting and free, if they are willing to toil with it. There is a land of sunshine and salt water, but some would have found it too hard to leave their television sets, to walk instead of ride, and now they are back with their chain stores and easy living, and I wonder if they are much better off.

Gus came over and took us to his house later on. There we met a married couple off the forty-foot 'Bojac', who were also sailing next day on their way back to the U.S. It was a good evening with plenty of laughter, and Gus outshone himself with his hospitality and Pepe with his cooking. We sailed at eight o'clock in the morning and when Gus came down to say good-bye he brought some bread and a cake to take with us. He stood on the wall in front of his house and watched our red sails fill as the wind took us out of the harbour.

There was a strong current against us most of the way to Santa Fe and not much light was left when we anchored. We had to shift the boat twice during the night as we dropped the hook too close inshore. In the morning, and during the next three days, we did not see one turtle in the bay, and most of the seals were gone from the beaches. While Duff and Bill caught and salted fish, I decided to do a little Stampiering myself. It is amazing what you will see if you look – and keep your eyes open. I had landed on the beach over a dozen times, built a fire to flatten the screwdriver, for a spear-head, on a rise covered in small bush and shrubs and saw nothing, but now, when I looked again, there was plenty to see.

A lot of old china was scattered about as well as pieces of hand-made bottles. The remains of over a dozen fireplaces lay around, some new, some almost buried. In several places there were signs of at least a semi-permanent camp with big, hollowed-out rocks being brought up and placed near the fireplace. Whether they were used to mix food in or to hold water I do not know. Flat slabs used for cutting up meat were close by. A clump of small trees turned out to be a circle of rocks placed there; how long ago it would be hard to judge, but the trees and shrubs have grown since then, their roots entwining through and around the stones.

As I did not have a shovel I could not dig much but, on scraping around under the flat slabs and inside the circle of stones, I found many pieces of old iron, so rusted that you could not tell what they were originally, and a few pieces of pottery. Some of these were very thin and blackened by age or fire. Some very thick pieces belonging to big water-jars had the finger-marks and print of the maker on the outside. Just what the circle of stones was built for in the first place can only be guessed at. It was eight foot long and six feet wide on the inside and stood four feet high and roughly three feet thick. Whalers could have built it for a shelter, or pirates could have used it for defence.

On one side of the bay close to the water stood three cairns of stones, seemingly put there without any reason, at least I could not see or think of any. Whether there was any connection between them and a small circle of reddish ground, mysteriously free of any rocks or stones close by, I do not know. The sun was too hot to feel like doing any digging. Having a good look around the bay, I decided to walk over the island to see if I could find any water, and set out early one morning. I dressed in shorts and sandshoes and took the spear with me in case I came across some goats.

Heading for a ridge, I crossed over fairly clear ground covered in small, dry, stunted shrubs. On a rise before the ridge I looked out over the water. The day was clear and I could see the island of San Cristobal clearly although it was nearly forty miles away. I was not the only one to stand and look over the same water, as many rocks had been placed for seats on the higher ground. Most of them were in pairs and had been built up with smaller stones to make them level. Some had been there for many years and were covered in lichen. I found only one fireplace here and it, too, had a flat stone alongside it. The only thing I saw that I could not understand was a rock twelve foot long and on its flat surface had been placed about two dozen small rocks and one flat one, in a dead-straight line.

At the foot of the ridge I came across the only place on the island that would hold water for any length of time. It was a deep fault in the rock, but like the rest of the island it, too, was dry. The ridge turned out to be just a narrow strip of all that was left of the solid rock – erosion had scattered the rest to form incredible rocky slopes on each side of it. From the top, the ridge led down to another bay not shown in the pilot book and charts. Although its sides were steep and rocky a patch of sand in the centre of it would make good anchoring. At the bottom I found old markers stuck in the rocks, probably used by the old whalers. This was an anchorage the sailing ships could sail out of, with the wind from all quarters.

It was here also that I saw the first mineral in a small reef that looked like feldspar. I continued following the valley inland for about half the island. In some places goat tracks were worn into the rock itself, and it was here that I saw two of them. Leaving this valley I crossed the ridge into a wider one, but before I was half-way across the rocks had cut the sandshoes off my feet. At the top, I came across another two goats and, after trying to catch one over the rocks, gave up when I almost broke my leg.

There were quite a few iguanas around here. A big one around four feet long was sitting on a rock in the sun. He took no notice of me as I set my camera up and took his photo. Having done this, we stood eyeing off each other. A goat walked up and stood in the shade of a cactus not ten yards from me.

Leaving these mounds I followed the dry creek-bed for a while. It was fine sand and gravel in which fine chips of black, volcanic rock sparkled in the sunlight. I crossed almost straight across the island until I reached the other coast, seeing nothing except iguanas and the bones of goats. In one place I came across the bones of two goats, their horns still locked in a battle that ended in death. Having no water with me, I tried some of the cactus pear and found they had plenty of moisture but were a little bitter, and the orange I had with me kept me going all day. Near the coast it was too rough for walking and I had to go back inland and follow a valley down to the boat. So thirsty was I when I reached the boat that I was not able to quench it for twenty-four hours.

There was a fair bit of dried fish on board and the only other thing we needed was cooking oil. As it was a dollar-and-a-half a bottle we decided to kill another seal and render the oil down on a fire ashore. We picked a fair-sized female who proved not at all easy to kill as she stood snarling and spitting. Duff was just a little faster with the axe than she was with her teeth and she went down with a sound that was almost human. Removing all the fat and meat, we took the carcass and dropped it into the sea from some rocks. Almost immediately a shark came nosing in, a big one around twelve feet long.

The seals shooting the breakers and playing in the water like a lot of happy children charged the shark as soon as it appeared. The smaller ones swam in circles around it while some of the larger males charged, trying to turn it, easily avoiding the shark when it swung towards them. However the smell of blood in the water was too strong and we watched the shark attack the carcass again and again, using its whole body as a lever to tear the meat free as it gripped the meat in his jaws. We took some good photos of the shark when Bill climbed down and held on to the skin of the seal while the shark churned up the water, thrashing and twisting, almost coming out of the water to tear the carcass free. We were all glad to see the last of it when it headed out to sea, the carcass held in its mouth like a dog holds a bone.

As soon as the shark disappeared, life went back to normal. Seals lolled and chased each other through the water, a pelican that was standing on a rock almost covered in bright red crabs, settled back on one leg and closed its eyes again. The half-dozen marine iguanas around its feet had not moved. The sun was too warm. A seal climbed laboriously over the rocks to peer with wrinkled brows at the smoke drifting lazily into the sky and to stare at the three figures almost asleep around the fire, lost interest and dived into the water with a splash.

For the three of us sitting around the fire, there could never be another place quite like these islands. I for one was reluctant to leave. Where else would you see so much life, find so much feeling. Even around our feet as we sat, there was life. Lizards of different colours and sizes scurried around, leaving their tracks in the red soil. Lift your eyes and you would look into those of a bird, staring down from a cactus covered in waxy, yellow flowers, but still, go we must – and with our six bottles of oil we rowed back out to the boat. We had never had so much food on board as we did just then, and never had we had such a rest in harbour. With a good night's sleep we were ready for the longest stretch of our trip: three-thousand-one-hundred miles to the islands of the Marquesas.

Chapter Fourteen

Galapagos to The Marquesas

We sailed next morning at nine o'clock. It was Monday, the last day in April. The fair wind we sailed with dropped at noon and we had light winds all afternoon and night. In the morning we were off Tortuga Island, about ten miles off Isabela, the largest in the group, and we were still off Isabela when the sun went down. We had put a message in a bottle over the side for Gus as we passed Santa Cruz. It was just as well we did it then, because when dawn came there was no sign of the islands, only a small seal swimming alone that seemed lost. We passed quite a few seals that day, most of them sleeping with their flippers stuck up in the air. The last group we saw were sixty miles from land.

We were able to put up our spinnakers the fourth day out but started rolling in the confused seas as soon as the fore-and-aft rig was down and had very little sleep. On the eighth day the wind swung around to the south-east and we steered under spinnakers to save our running rigging, until the twelfth day. We then hoisted our fore-and-aft sails again as we ran into strong winds and squalls. We were glad of the change as it looked like being a long, drawn-out trip. Some days we logged only fifty or sixty miles in twenty-four hours. Our run for the next day was one-hundred-and-eighty miles and, together with the next four days, we ran seven-hundred-and-thirty miles. This, of course, was with the current to help us along.

Spearfishing, Pacific Ocean.

Fish were with us most of the way. One night we caught something big but it smashed up the big line as though it was cotton. The loss of the big harpoon was a setback to us, and when using the light one out of the spear gun we lost the dropper off it so Duff got to work and made another out of a five-franc piece. We caught quite a few fish on this before one took the spear, and the last of our broom handles with it, then Duff used his lines.

Most of the fish we caught were salted down in their own brine and kept in a bucket. We ate this fish for breakfast every morning and, when it was washed and cooked properly, it was hard to tell the difference from fresh fish. There was a school of Dorado alongside for many hundreds of miles. At night they would come in and get drawn along with the suction of the boat with very little effort on their part, and we could lean over the side and almost touch them. Slowly, Duff caught them one by one until only the 'Veteran', as we nicknamed him, was left. He swam alongside us day after day, showing no effect of the five harpoon wounds we had given him.

He seemed to realise the harpoon was gone and would swim about four feet from the side, leaving it only to chase flying-fish. This he did with great ferociousness, sometimes leaving the water and catching them in the air. He ignored Duff's lures after he had inspected them once. This, of course, made Duff very unhappy and more and more determined to catch him. The thing he had made out of wood and painted silver was the only lure that took the 'Veteran' by surprise. He charged in and snapped. I grimaced as his teeth bit into the wood. I never saw a more surprised fish as he swam away, presumably spitting out wood or teeth. He swam back to inspect this strange thing, and did so thoroughly. After that he would not give it so much as a glance.

The battle between these two took up much of Duff's spare time and became such an obsession that I was glad when the fish disappeared. Secretly I hoped he would not be caught, but Duff would stand on deck and watch the 'Veteran' for minutes on end, like a cat watching a mouse, his eyes following every move, every swish of its tail, while his mind planned. When his latest idea would fail, and the fish swim away untouched, I thought he would blow his top as he stood there, clenching and unclenching his fists, teetering on his toes, almost ready to dive in after it and catch it with his bare hands.

Time passed quickly and the days seemed to fly. I had plenty of typing to do as I was still back in the West Indies with my notes. The sights every day took up a fair bit of time, with Bill taking them and then the three of us working out and plotting them on the chart. That way we checked each other for mistakes, and every day the crosses moved slowly across the chart. The rest of the time we read books or caught up on some of the sleep we lost on watches. Cooking filled in quite a bit of time. None of us was bored. In fact, some days it was hard to find enough time to do everything we wished to do.

After these strong winds we had three days of light winds and tried using our spinnakers again, but we all woke up with such sore backs through not being able to relax we were only too pleased to go back to the fore-and-aft rig. We made far better speed under it also. The rest of the trip was really wonderful sailing, with the wind blowing steadily day and night. The days were beautiful, clear and mild, the sun coming up astern in the morning and going down ahead in the afternoon. At night we sailed along under a star-filled sky. The only thing breaking the serenity of these nights were the shooting stars that flashed across the sky, some incredibly brilliant. They would light the sky with a bluish glow and give you a feeling of awe before they burnt themselves out and disappeared, leaving you with a strange feeling of emptiness or loss.

On the twenty-ninth we had very strong winds and had to reef the main a little. There were plenty of seagulls around and our sight that day gave us sixty-five miles to run to the first island. With strong winds and big seas behind us, we ran our distance on the log by four in the morning and, with no sign of the island, we hove-to until daylight. When it showed up six miles away we were fifteen miles off our course. Whether it was our sights or the current, I do not know. The wind was still strong, and as there was no chance of tacking back against it to the main harbour of Taio Hae, we headed for the nearest island we could see.

Our gear, which had been slowly deteriorating, started to break. First to go was a bolt in the gaff boom. Luckily it went in daylight, and we had another bolt of the same size to take its place. One of the halyards parted and, almost at the same time, one of the after-stays went with a crack like a whip. After fixing up everything temporarily, we tried to start the motor and it took half an hour to kick over due to condensation. We were close inshore by now and had to throw a tack back out to sea while Duff got stuck into the motor. The island of Nuku Hiva was a high, rugged one with tall, limestone cliffs through which high waterfalls had cut their course.

Around the coast in front of us, pinnacles of rock in fantastic shapes and sizes stood majestically above the sea which pounded them and threw spray high into the air. From where we were we could see three bays, and as soon as the motor was going we dropped our sails and headed towards the largest of them. Plantations of coconut palms lined the slopes at the head of the bay. All the ridges had been cleared, leaving the scars to stand out from the green.

Even before we turned into the bay we could see the 'sentinels', as I called them, standing on a ridge on the right of the village. These three pillars of rock towered over the tiny buildings and stood apart, like lofty giants, from the rest of the surrounding country. The bay ran in quite a way and had deep water almost up to the stony beach. Standing out in the centre of the village, the first building we could see was the church, its two steeples marking it as French. We steered for this on our way in and dropped anchor in two fathoms of water. Most of the houses in the village were built of iron. Only a few were made out of plaited fibre with palm-frond roofs. It turned out to be the harbour of Hatiheu and we were in calm water again after a fairly good trip of thirty days, an average of a little over a hundred miles a day.

That night we slept the sleep of dead men, and in the morning we started to repair the gear and get the boat ready for sea again. Our water had lasted well, and we used the last of our main tank this day and took our cans over to a tap on a small wharf, tipped the brackish water out and filled them with the best water we had drunk since Vigo, in Spain. One of the islanders came out to the boat in his canoe and tried to sell us a beautiful, hand-carved dish. We finished up making a deal with him for some bananas, papaw and coconuts and gave him a bottle of rum. Although we told him to bring them next day, he had one look at the rum and was back in an hour with his horse loaded with fruit.

Just after dark that night he came back with a mate, and quite a bit of the rum inside him. They came on board with their ukuleles and, although we did not feel like it, sang song for song with them until well into the night. Duff made a big hit with his hillbilly songs and they tagged him with the name 'Cowboy'. When we turned in they slept on the double mattress on the floor. The next day we had a visit from the chief, a big, stocky man and, as we knew no French and he no English, there was not much we could say to each other. He had brought along a young boy who could speak a bit of English and, through him, we learnt that the chief was not very happy at all. I don't think it was because we had pulled in there, but the fact that we did not have a clearance from the main port of Taio Hae. We explained about the wind and our broken gear, not forgetting to add that our water was low, and we asked if we could stay another five days. He agreed, as long as we typed out the name of the boat and just why we did not go to Taio Hae. With this in his hand he got back in his canoe and returned to shore.

It was not until the fourth day we went ashore and had a look at the village. It was spotlessly clean and tidy with hand-made tracks and roads running through it. There was a fair-sized store run by the inevitable Chinese. You could buy everything from tinned food to clothes. There was even a refrigerator for cold Coca-Cola and beer. Most of the people were reasonably well-off, exporting copra and coffee to Tahiti, and quite a few owned the big, outboard motors for their boats and canoes. The fishing was very poor and the few who went spear-fishing spent hours in the water for little reward. This did not stop one old native by the name of Pio trying to give us three crayfish, and in the end we gave him four ounces of tobacco for them.

He then took us to his house, which was a little way inland. For quite a way we walked along a track about six feet wide that had been built up with stones first and then covered with soil. When we left it, the track carried on to another village three miles away. Around his house were trees of almost every kind of fruit and he filled a sack for us with mangoes, papaw, limes and oranges, and showed us everything that grew there. His taro patch was quite big, and it was the first time I had seen it growing. We stopped there for an hour before making our way back to the boat along another track.

As Bill could not dive any more, because of his ears, Duff spent a fair bit of time fishing with the natives and had the experience of helping to remove a fair-sized octopus from one of them. Our friendly native, Pio, speared it in a hole. It shot out, swam up the spear and pinioned his arms. As Duff was closest he swam out and tried to pull it off by putting one foot in the middle of its back, but it was only with the help of another native that they managed to get it off and into the canoe. Everyone spent the next five minutes laughing, taking it all as a big joke. We lived mainly on a diet of fruit while we were there. It was certainly good to eat, but it did terrible things to our stomachs.

I did not go off the boat again. We had thought about going over to Taio Hae on horseback. The two dollars they wanted for a horse would have stopped us, but time was the main problem. We just could not go away and leave the boat. We spent six days there altogether. It was a wonderful rest and one we needed. After six days we were as fit as ever, and sailed on the sixth of June for Takaroa, a trip of four-hundred-and-fifty miles. Down the coast we had good wind but lost it in the lee, and did not have it again until it came up from the south-east when the sun went down.

Chapter Fifteen

The Marquesas to Tuamotu Archipelago

We had beautiful weather all the way. For the first four days the wind was fair and, just when it looked like we would make a fast trip, the wind fell slowly off. On the twelfth we had no wind all night and logged only ten miles. I had the morning watch and, at dawn, climbed up the mast and sighted the island of Takaroa about fifteen to twenty miles away. It looked like a few sticks on the horizon and was not visible from the deck until almost noon. There was very little wind and we started the motor at five o'clock to get into the harbour before dark, but the island seemed to have no end to it. We sighted the wreck we had been looking for, as a landmark, just on dark and, with Bill up the mast, we looked for the entrance.

It was just as well there was a little moonlight when we reached the passage through the reef, as it was not very wide. We were lucky to have the tide on the first of the ebb on our way in, and, although Bill could see the reefs from the masthead, my throat was a little dry before we were safely through and heading for the wharf. Quite a crowd was there to take our lines and a lot of laughing and talking went on before we finally tied up. Again we could not understand any of the language, and were lucky there was a Mormon missionary visiting the island so we could tell everyone where we were from and where we were going.

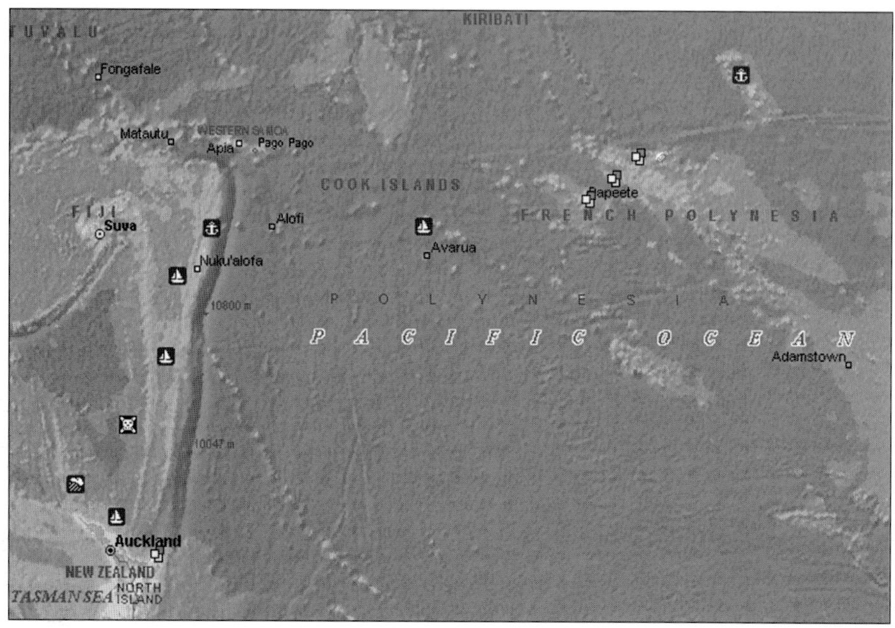

Marquesas to New Zealand.

Alongside the wharf it was dead flat and was the quietest we had laid for many months. Even our canary sang longer and louder. In the morning it felt great to wake up after a good night's sleep and look out over the lagoon at the palm-covered atoll. It had taken us long enough to reach here. There were plenty of fish just off the wharf in the clear water, so we would have no worries about food. The village was nearly empty as most of the people were away on the islands around the lagoon getting copra. Many of those who were there came down to have a look at the boat and say hello.

The children especially were at the boat whenever they got a chance – not to look at us, but at the canary. There were no birds on the island and his singing amazed them. It took us a while to get used to seeing heads peering into the boat from every scuttle. The island was very pretty but there were not many trees. The village was tidy, and even the road running through it was raked every day. Most of the people were Mormons and we did not see any of the hulas you hear about, I think Duff played the guitar and sang more than anyone. Everyone was very friendly and Duff went spear-fishing quite a few times with some of the young blokes. If someone went out and brought back a few clams they always made sure we got some.

The thirty-six-foot yacht, 'Who Goes There' arrived the day after us and tied up close by. It belonged to an American who would have been in his sixties. He sailed alone from Panama and had missed the Galapagos Islands because of the currents. He had a very long trip to the Marquesas, taking eighty days, and had to distil water for drinking along the way. For the trip to Tahiti he had two men on board whom he had picked up in Nuku Hiva. One of them knew the star sight we wanted to learn and, although they only stayed one day and night, we were able to pick it up. The skipper was quite a character, wore an old lap-lap and chewed tobacco. He had all new rigging on his boat and gave us a long length of the old stuff to replace some of ours which was worn. When they sailed they had a good wind that put their masthead down on the horizon within a few hours.

We stayed on this island four days, and for every one of them the weather was beautiful. On the last night we went over to the house of the island's radio operator. He was a Tahitian and could speak a little English. The collection of shells that filled his house was really something to see. Duff had his guitar with him and we sang quite a few songs which the radio operator taped on his recorder.

We sailed at ten the next morning and got away with a good wind. Looking back, the island was very pretty as it dropped astern. The wind fell off during the afternoon and at sundown there was very little. The island of Manihi showed itself at dawn, about six miles away on our beam. We were about six miles off course and a lot further ahead than our log registered. We started to run down the length of the island at nine o'clock and, with very little wind all day, had to start our motor at four in the afternoon. We ran through the reef at about five o'clock without any trouble. The wharf was a lot smaller than Takaroa, and again there were plenty of people to take the lines. As soon as we were secure the boat was invaded. The decks and cabin were crowded. No-one left when we started cooking but watched everything we cooked and how we did it.

That night there was a hula. The people all sat around a very old tree with big spreading branches and danced and sang for over four hours. They were practising their dances and songs for the tourists who arrived by seaplane once a week. After practice was finished they continued to sing and danced the hula for quite a while. Even Duff and I were up doing it, not that we needed too much encouragement, especially Duff, who was like a greyhound after a rabbit. It didn't do either of us any good, however, as we found that, contrary to what is written and usually believed, the morals of the people here and in Takaroa were above reproach. The young people practised hard at their dances and lifted their voices to harmonise this sad, haunting music. The young children fell asleep on their mats around the big tree to the sound of the songs, and the old people sitting in the background joined in or sat quietly, remembering when they, too, twisted and danced around the circle with swaying hips and flashing smiles, their eyes challenging the men to a dance that always ended in laughter.

We stayed on the island of Manihi for three days and it was beautiful weather all the time. The main reason we did not stay longer was the anchorage. It was terrible, with swells sometimes three-feet high lifting and throwing the boat around, breaking our ropes, even though we had our two anchors out holding us off the wall. Then the coral cut our inch-thick anchor rope twice. We had to use rope instead of our chain which was much too heavy. The people were very friendly and there was always plenty of fish to eat as the young men went out every day and would not come back without seeing we had some. Duff went out a few times with them. Quite a few sharks were around and he had three fish taken off the end of his spear.

The island itself was prettier than Takaroa, having more trees and flowers. As the pearl-diving season was finished there was very little for the men to do. They worked their copra when it had to be done, and practised spear-throwing for the benefit of the tourist. They were very good at this. Throwing at a coconut on a high pole a hundred yards away, it was amazing the number of hits they got. I even tried my hand at it, and although I did not get any hits I got a lot of laughs.

We decided to sail on Friday the twenty-second of June and go straight to Tahiti. One of the young men dived down and brought up our anchors, breathing with a particular whistling sound before he dived. He was under the water for over a minute-and-a-half picking up one of the anchors and walking it along the bottom.

A number of people came on board to say good-bye before we sailed. One of them was Perry, a bloke from the next island of Ahe and he could speak a little English. He asked us to come over to his island and was very surprised when we said that we were going straight to Tahiti. He was one of the chiefs, or governors, on the island, and offered to give us five gallons of petrol as well as a chicken dinner that night and, although we said no to the petrol, we could not very well say no to the chicken.

We sailed at nine-thirty with a fair wind and, although we were doing a good speed by our standards, I think that the chief found it a little slow, as he liked to use his fast outboard. He told us a little about the pearl diving. The divers rotated around the different islands, coming back to each one every few years. The pearl-diving season lasts three months, and during that time about three thousand people dive, including women and children, who sometimes got shell from the shallow water. A good diver can earn up to three thousand American dollars during these few months. They are paid by the kilo and a good diver can bring up between fifty and eighty kilos a day. If he is lucky enough to find a pearl, he has struck the jackpot. One man told us he had brought up seven shells and had got seven pearls. His karma was good. I do not know the average depth that they can dive, but I was told they can go down eighty to one hundred feet on occasions.

On our way over to Ahe we had a good chance to tend our boils and sores that were starting to break out. The scurvy of the old sailing ships was beginning to catch up with us – perhaps it was the length of time we had been at sea plus the lack of fresh fruit and vegetables. The Barcoo rot in the bush in Australia looked the same. It may have been as simple as getting coral into cuts and scratches, thereby forming ulcers. Because of these lesions we began taking some of the vitamin pills we had brought onboard in England, even though they may have been outdated by now. We were only half-way to Ahe when the chief started to feel unwell, he did not like the motion of the boat and slept the rest of the way.

We picked up a good wind about midday and came up on the island very fast. The only difference between it and the other islands was that it appeared to have more sand and more beaches. Perry guided us through the reef, which was just as well as the passage was very narrow. Had we been coming in by ourselves, we would have turned back when we saw the rollers ahead of us. It looked as if there was a reef right across the entrance and, when we passed over it, we were thrown around quite a bit before our boat cut through into the calm water of the lagoon. The main island was about three miles away, with markers on all the shallow coral. Unfortunately, there was only three feet of water alongside the small jetty, so we dropped anchor in ten feet of water with hardly a ripple on it and which was sheltered by a small island.

Ahe looked more natural than many other places, with more grass huts along the shore. It was prettier than the other islands because it had retained more top-soil, whereas the others were almost bare coral. As we stepped onto the jetty to go to Perry's house, these friendly people placed rings of flowers around our necks. This made Bill very happy, as at last something had happened that followed the pattern of the books he had read as a young boy, and his dream to see these South Sea Islands had been fulfilled. We had a very good meal of wonderfully cooked chicken. When these people eat they certainly enjoy their food, and when we left the table we were just about bursting.

Before we went back to the boat for the night, Perry asked us to come for coffee in the morning and sent his boat to get us. It was our first taste of how they made coffee in these islands black and so strong that you could stand a spoon up in it. When our coffee was finished, Perry showed us around the island which was home to about one-hundred-and-fifty people and, although it was small, there was everything growing here. Most of the trees and hedges had been systematically planted with a lot of thought and foresight. A new school was being built of brick and cement, and a number of men were working on it while some were away working on copra.

The island people went out of their way to help us and would not let us eat onboard. When it was meal-time someone would come down to the boat and ask us to come to his house. These people did not get any tourists, as planes did not stop here and yachts were few and far between. We were the first to call in six months.

Bill was sick the day after we arrived and decided to stay in his bunk. Unfortunately, he missed the big dinner these lovely people put on for us in the school. The long table was loaded with food: fish, salads, big plates of rice, chicken done with peas, roast pork, poi, etc. There were two kinds of fish, soaked in lime juice and covered in grated coconut, also baked and mashed breadfruit that tasted ten times better than we had ever cooked. Then, in case you were still hungry, there was plenty of cake and fruit juice. Duff, a very small eater, was full in no time, but I managed to put a fair bit away, with nods of approval from all the old men who enjoyed the food as much as we did. There were speeches after the meal, and I could only reply with a word or two that I had picked up. That night, nearly all the young men mustered at the wharf and sang songs for a long time, with Duff joining in with his cowboy songs.

We decided to wait until Bill was better before we sailed, so Duff and I agreed to give the men a hand mixing cement at the new school. The work was not very hard, and the fact that we helped them endeared us to the people even more. It became impossible to eat onboard at all. If we cooked a meal they would come out to the boat, wait until we had finished eating, and then take us ashore and give us another meal. Every family waited its turn for the day to come when we would eat at their house and they spent hours preparing and cooking the native dishes. They laughed at us for doing our own washing, and they asked us to take it ashore for the women to wash and iron.

It was four days before Bill was able to get out of his bunk and feel well enough to do a bit of work on board. Duff and I worked at the school and got a lot of laughs between us as we tried to pick up the language. When Saturday came, we took as many as our boat would hold over to the pass for fishing. We all had a wonderful day swimming around in the shallow water and diving down around the coral looking for shells. The few sharks that were there did not bother us at all, and the men got plenty of fish with their spears on the outside of the reef. Duff cooked a meal onboard, which was quite a feat, and the pancakes were well received. We did the trip back under sail, though I think most of them found it a little slow. In my experience not many people have the patience for sailing.

The next day being a Sunday, the three of us decided to muster to church for the first time in a long while. We decided to go to the Mormon church in the morning and then to the main church, the Sanito, that night. We knew this would make every-one happy, as they took their religion very seriously. They were a bit concerned about me as I told them I was a heathen, and they believed that I would go straight to hell. I guess I should have told them that I had little time for organised religions, as my beliefs are that there are no religions higher than truth. The Mormon church was a thatched building; and I don't know if they thought we needed it or that it was too good a chance to miss, but they held three services at the one time and took two hours. There was a young Mormon missionary from America present, and he explained to us what was going on. I found that it was easier to think of different religions as stars in the sky: some are like black holes that suck in people and give no light, some give a little light, while others give a great deal of light, but without any light there would only be darkness. At night we went to the Sanito hall. It was a fairly laid-back affair with a lot of singing accompanied by guitars and the three of us enjoyed it. Most of the children were asleep around the hall, with the old men nodding their heads before it was finished. It was a simple meeting and one that you could not help but like.

The next day the three of us were at work on the school, Duff swinging a paint brush, Bill plastering, and I was stuck on the end of a shovel. The new paint on the school looked a first-class job, and a credit to the men working on it as none of them had any training at all. Most of the accolades must go to the man in charge, a quiet French Tahitian, with much patience, who built schools and hospitals around most of the islands. His wife could not do enough for us, as her father was an Australian. She must have been taught to cook by her Tahitian mother as her food was out of this world. Duff, who ate only as much as a four-year-old boy, would get a hard look and her fist would be shaken at him, when he would say he was full half way through the meal.

It did not matter where we ate. If it was the chief's house, or the poorest house on the island made of thatch with a sand floor, they all said the same thing, eat until you are full, and the more you ate the better they liked you. The three of us worked on the school until Wednesday. We spent almost every night at the house of Hitinui, a tall Tuamotuan with a great sense of humour. He was trying to learn English and picked up our way of speech very quickly, certainly a lot faster than I picked up Tahitian, but somehow we always managed to understand each other. Hitinui's wife was due to have her baby, and she was happy to name it after one of us should it be a boy. There was no doctor on the island and the only thing we could do to help was to give her a bottle of rum, as they like to have a drink to put them to sleep after the baby arrives, even though it is against their religion and they would not touch it any other time.

As there are no minerals in the soil on the island many of the people had bad teeth, and there was not even a pair of tooth-pulling pliers in the village. A man came up to me his face white with pain. He was holding a pair of pliers in his hand and he begged me to pull his tooth out. I took him out to the boat, along with a Tahitian missionary who could speak a little English. The only association he had with a dentist was that his father always carried a pair of pulling pliers around in his back pocket while doing the rounds of the islands. We sat our patient down on a bucket and poured boiling water over the small pliers we used for the motor. When they were cool enough I tried to pull the tooth out with a straight pull. The pliers kept slipping off, and I would not move the tooth sideways for fear of it breaking off. I did not have the strength to make any impact so I handed over to the sixteen-stone Tahitian while I held our patient's head pressing on his temples. The agony that he went through was showing in his eyes but he did not make a sound. The Tahitian was doing his best with an almost-useless tool. He braced himself, sweat rolling down his face, his muscles bulging with the effort, and suddenly the tooth came out nice and clean. I don't know who was more relieved, me or the victim. Bill, who had watched in silence, had the look on his face that told me I would never get the pliers in his mouth. The tooth had a hole in it and could have been filled. Our patient rinsed his mouth in salt water and thanked us very much and, as we rowed him ashore, he told us that all the pain had gone.

We told our friends we would be sailing next day and they insisted that we should have another feast before we left. The women were busy cooking and getting bread-fruit. The heads of chickens were disappearing at an alarming rate, and the old sow was looking in vain for her missing piglet.

On our last day on the island, Duff made one last try to win a girl that he had his eyes on – 'faint heart never smacked fair bottom'. He was scheming for days how to take her out for a walk. Her mother, Rangi, was the biggest woman on the island and one of the happiest. Her weight would make any set of scales shake in terror, and she looked as if she could crack peanuts with her eyelashes. I could see that she did not trust either of them – any time they managed to be alone it was only a matter of minutes before someone turned up. To court a girl on the island was a very complicated and hazardous affair. The girl hoped, if not expected, that the boy friend should find his way to her house, making sure which bed was hers, then climb through the window and join her in the sack. Of course, before he could hope to do this, there was a little matter of making friends with about one hundred dogs so he could move around freely after dark. If he should get caught climbing through the window, or in the room, there would be much embarrassment when pointed out to the laughing villagers. With a twenty-stone mother, who slept across the doorway, there were not many young blokes, including Duff, who were willing to take the risk. I shuddered at the thought of what she may have done to his 'family jewels' should she have woken up as he was stepping over her. I had seen how she had crushed a coconut and was impressed. Duff finally fronted up to mum and asked if they could go for a walk. Getting the nod, they set off happily up the road with an escort of half the children on the island twenty yards behind. I didn't like his chances.

Farewell from the people of Ahe.

Bill wandered around having his last look at the island, while I was content to sit in the shade of a breadfruit tree and chew the fat with anyone who came along. The long table had been laid for the feast, so I brought a bottle of rum from the boat for any of the old men who would like a nip. However, as soon as 'twenty stoner' saw it her big hand removed it from the table and dropped it down between her ample bosom, which would have concealed a five-gallon keg without much trouble. That was the last I saw of it until it turned up on the table, wonderfully mixed with fruit juice. The feast was a great success, though I did not get to taste any dog, which they favour above all other meat, bearing in mind that these dogs only eat coconut. The raw fish soaked in lime and rolled in grated coconut was a delight to the palate and one of my favourites. The rum punch gave that little spark that livened things up.

We were going to sail around lunch-time but, at 3 o'clock in the afternoon we were still eating; then the guitars came out and the singing started. It was unthinkable that we should sail that day. We sang all afternoon until coffee that night and then, after finishing the last of the rum punch, Duff and Bill kept them in fits of laughter half the night, doing the hula and putting on a few acts of their own. I refused to do the hula unless some of the girls got up. They couldn't do this as it was against their church teachings, so I ended up doing a Maori haka up and down the hall a couple of times. While all this noise was going on a woman gave birth to a baby boy in a little grass hut across the road, and its first misfortune in life would be to be named after one of us.

The next day Rangi was out at our boat, asking us to have dinner at her place even before we were out of bed. It could take a week to leave a place like this. Many of the people asked us to stay until Sunday and were disappointed when we said we had to go. I find it hard to say good-bye to someone I care about and I had one hell of a time saying farewell to fifty. All that morning people kept giving us shells, sometimes it was young girls whose heads only reached up to our waist, or some of the young boys who almost wore out our oars rowing our dinghy around the sheltered waters inside the reef. People would stop and say good-bye with real sadness in their eyes.

The dinner was marvellous, and once again Rangi made sure we had plenty to eat. When the meal was finished she gave us a letter to her father in Tahiti, asking him to look after us and show us around. Her husband wanted to give us a letter to take to an office in Tahiti so we would get paid for the work we had done on the school, but we explained that we would not have worked for money. Then he gave us a letter stating that we had worked there, which we all agreed to keep as a souvenir. Quite a few of the people gave us letters to take to Tahiti and I suspect some of them were to friends asking them to keep an eye on us. We started off at the new school saying our good-byes and worked our way around the houses. By the time we reached the wharf our necks were so loaded with shell necklaces and rings of flowers it was an effort to hold our heads up. Then came the good part. We had to kiss the women good-bye, first on one cheek and then the other, and there were a great many of them aged from six to sixty. I noticed that they planted their kisses on Bill's forehead to dodge his beard. Duff and I had shaved ours off not long after we arrived, not that it did me much good and Duff wasn't talking. When we finally got into the dinghy and shoved off, there were quite a few moist eyes, including Hitinui.

It was 3 o'clock before we got underway and turned our bow seaward. The memory of Ahe and its people will last in our hearts forever. It will be there when we are tired and depressed, and when we are cold and wet at the helm. If the rest of the trip holds nothing, at least there will be the memory of this one little island.

Chapter Sixteen

Tuamotus to Tahiti

We were thrown around quite a bit going through the reef and cleared it around four o'clock. We picked up a good wind that pushed us along a hundred miles in the first twenty-four hours. It was only the next day that we realised we had unwittingly sailed on a Friday. I am not too superstitious, but I would not have knowingly disregarded such a long-standing belief as this one. I felt a little sea-sick for the first time – perhaps it was the big dinner or the rum I had consumed the day before. The next day I felt fine again. Our run of one hundred miles carried our boat well clear of the Tuamotus.

We sighted the island of Rangiroa at dawn. On our beam, about six miles away, we could see a number of strong squalls heading our way. The first one hit us with such force that I gybed the main and one of the bolts broke on the side of the gaff. Again we were fortunate that Bill had put a spare one onboard and he repaired it in about five minutes. The wind died away that night and for two days we had light winds and calm seas. The wind was changing direction time and time again, and there were more strong squalls that brought the rain down in bucket loads.

Duff sighted Tahiti at sundown on the 9th with its cloud-piercing peaks, and we lay becalmed all that night and the next day. To add to our woes we ran out of cigarette paper and none could be found after almost turning the boat upside-down. Duff started to smoke toilet paper, while I settled for writing paper. There was nothing that we could do, we just sat and waited. Slowly, slowly our boat moved closer to the island and then, on the 11th, a good wind carried us right up. The light on Point Venus started to flash at sundown as we moved along the coast. Without a pilot book we did not know how far the reef was from the land, so we trusted our luck and kept a good lookout. We picked up the first of the green leading-lights at nine o'clock, passed through the reef half an hour later and then steered into the harbour by the second lot of lights. There were about twenty yachts tied up against the wall, so we motored around until we found a vacant place, went in, dropped our anchor and fell back on it. We tied the stern to the wall and went to sleep thinking about the fire-works that would start in the morning.

The gendarme was there about eight o clock and looked like a man who had just stood on a green bull-ants nest, his arms waving in the air. He was red in the face and there was no way that I could understand him. Bill came on deck and in no time grasped the situation. All the gendarme was worried about was that we had come into harbour without paying our pilot fee. Bill did his best to calm the troubled waters and agreed to go ashore and pay the fee. Although we had very little money left, we did not have a choice.

Tahiti is a very beautiful island, and we were glad to step ashore and look around Papeete. At first we were mystified why there were so many people about, then we learned that most of them were there to celebrate the 14th July, Bastille Day. Polynesians had come from many of the small villages and the surrounding islands, some from where we had just come, the Tuamotus, Tonga, Rarotonga, Huahine, Raietea. They came from all over the South Pacific to take part and compete in the island games. Some of their canoe races were great to watch.

We needed money in a place like this, so it was decided to use our 'international currency' and sold one of the two cases of scotch whiskey we had put on board before we left England. At least we could be kings for a day or two. Duff headed off to the market to buy fresh fish and fruit while Bill and I wandered around the many colourful stalls that had been set up for the occasion. We went into one of the bars that was open for business to cater for those who liked a drop of the amber fluid. The beer tasted like someone had tipped a bag of onions into it, but I knew that I could get to like it with a little practice. Bill was not so sure, still the company was good and they were a happy group. Someone produced a guitar and in no time the sound of the beautiful Polynesian songs drifted out across the bay, harmonising as only Polynesians can.

Time stood still for a little while, and then it was back to the boat. Bill and I watched Duff coming towards the boat carrying his market purchases. He had a look on his face like the cat that had just caught the canary, and I wondered why. As he got closer I realised he had two or three Tahitian lasses with him. Duff explained they had helped him buy local food at the market and were happy to show him how to cook it, so it looked as if we were going to eat well, and we might also have dessert!

It was a beautiful sunset that night, but our peace and tranquillity was shattered, not only that night but every night. Our boat was between two bands playing loud and long into the early hours of the morning, and the three of us could not wait to get back to sea, but the wind would have none of that and we waited ten long days for it to change. It was not all bad, at least we could go for a walk around. I have seen a lot of beautiful women around the world, some it was their eyes, some it was their voice, but the Chinese-Tahitians with their long, black hair got ten out of ten from me.

The longer we stayed in Papeete the less money we had. There were times when the three of us sat in the cockpit looking at our neighbours on the yacht 'Faith' who looked as if they had more money than God, but their youth was gone, so we sat side by side pondering on our lot. Perhaps the Buddhist saying, 'all is impermanent' is true, it certainly is with youth and money. From time to time the Tahitian lasses called into our boat. I did not know if it was to hear our canary sing, or to see us or perhaps it was the food, it really did not matter as they brightened up our day and were welcome. Finally the wind changed. That was our first bit of good luck, the second was that twenty-five pounds that had been following Bill around the world caught up with him just at the right time and he shared his good luck with us. Duff was off to the market for supplies and I could see a spring in his step. Bill got the boat ready and I filled the water tanks.

On the 19th of July, Bill went around to the port officials to tell them we wanted to sail the next day and paid our port dues. He was told an official would be down at the wharf at ten o'clock. The wind in the harbour was blowing from everywhere so it was hard to tell its true direction. The other New Zealand yacht, the 'Faith', was also getting ready to sail, but she was headed for Samoa instead of Fiji. At least we would both be on the same course for a while.

That night I did my usual three times around the stall area. The Chinese were still going strong with their gambling wheels and the smell of the roasting pig and beef wafted out among the crowd to join the many smells of the area. The dance bands were still trying unsuccessfully to drown one another out. I watched the hula dancing for a while, or at least tried to. The crowd was so large that the only part I saw clearly was when the tall men and women from Bora Bora left the area with proudly lifted heads and swaying grass skirts. Finally, I found my way back to my favourite little bar, propped myself up against the same tree and settled back to enjoy a beer, which I hoped I could make last for an hour or so.

I was still on the same bottle when I spotted Bill and Duff picking their way through the crowd. Bill had his pipe in his mouth and his hands clasped behind his back, as if he was Officer of the Watch on a quarter-deck. Both had their eyes glued to the ground, no doubt hoping that someone had just dropped a wallet. Joining me at the table we pooled our money, enabling us to have another bottle each, so we settled back to watch the people flow by. The old Tahitian with his bad leg was still limping past with monotonous regularity holding the kicking, squealing piglets that seemed to come from an inexhaustible supply. I noticed that he, too, like the flowers and the palm fronds, had wilted a little since the start of the celebrations.

There was still a continuous stream of beautiful girls passing, at whom Duff bared his teeth occasionally, but they were just out of biting distance from our table. My lass, Huria, had disappeared from onboard early in the morning and apparently decided to do something about my suggestion of finding someone with plenty of money, or perhaps she was just hungry. She turned up soon after I had started on the second bottle of beer, with three Tahitians in tow, and was she loaded!

Huria had three sarongs draped around her neck, all different colours, there was a five-pointed deputy-sheriff's badge as big as a plate pinned on her coat, one ring of flowers on her head and another around her neck. Dropping down in a chair next to me, she began to count her loot, dance tickets, raffle tickets and as drunk as she was I don't think she missed any. Watching me out of the corner of her eye to see what my reaction would be, she pulled out a wad of hundred-franc notes that made Bill and Duff's eyes water. As there was no comment from me, Huria suggested that she and I should go and paint the place red, the cars, the speed-boats, the works. After thinking it over I decided she would have more fun without me, as no amount of urging would get me up to do the 'Twist', and I had no intention of getting drunk the night before sailing. I shook my head, feeling like a real party-pooper. She looked at me a little reproachfully before buying me another beer, and weaved her way through the crowd in the general direction of the cars, leaving me to finish my beer and wonder if it pays to have too many principles.

I never really expected Huria to come back onboard, but she arrived as usual – so drunk by then that it will always remain a mystery just how she managed to walk over the six-inch gangway. She dropped into the cabin of our boat like a bomb, right on top of our two Tuamotuan friends who were sleeping on the floor. Before I was fully awake she had kicked them off the boat and left them shivering in the cold. She then woke up Duff and Bill and explained to the three of us that she, being a Marquesan, had no time for men from the Tuamotus, then passed out on the spot. Our two friends were then able to come back onboard for the rest of the night. The sound of Huria snoring kept most of us awake, and in the morning I watched her as she woke up, trying not to smile at the look on her face as she studied the English tweed coat she could not remember getting, and the five-star badge. Before she could work everything out, the mental strain was interrupted by the delayed hangover and she began eating Aspros like Minties. I made her breakfast and we said our good-byes. After all, there was a boat to get ready.

It was time to leave Tahiti and, with the stern lines onboard and the old motor coughing out rings of black smoke, Bill and Duff took up the slack on the anchor chain as I pushed the gear handle in with my foot. Pushing the throttle down we shot away from the wall, a little too fast for the crew of the 'Faith' who ran along their boat ready in case we should take off a little of their newly scrubbed paintwork, but they could have saved themselves the exercise as we went out cleanly. I breathed a sigh of relief when our anchor broke out clean and did not foul in the maze of ropes and anchors laid out ahead of us. I only looked back once to see if I could make out the long-haired Marquesan lass among the crowd waiting for the 'Faith' to sail, but she was gone. We were then swinging around, lining up the markers, and the boom swung out under the pressure of the slowly filling sail. We heeled over slightly and ran along the calm waters inside the reef.

Chapter Seventeen

Tahiti to Tonga

It was a beautiful day and, for the first time since we arrived, we could see the rugged beauty of the hills around Tahiti etched against the blue of the sky. We had not even cleared the narrow passage through the reef before the cross-seas of the new wind rushed to meet us and we were rolling and yawing on the first part of our trip to Fiji. The confused wind around the island headed us off instead of helping us, and before we had gone a quarter of a mile we pulled in our flogging sails and wildly swinging booms and continued on under motor hoping for a wind that would carry us clear. The yacht 'Faith' overhauled us easily half-way between Tahiti and the island of Moorea and, although she was rolling much more than us, it was not hard to see the advantage of her modern lines and easily driven hull. As we got closer to Moorea we ran into a patch of strong current and choppy seas that reminded us we had spent a little too long in harbour. The change of wind we were hoping for still had not come.

As we were running down the coast of the small island the sun was getting low in the sky and, rather than spend the night rolling our guts out in the heavy swell, we pointed closer to shore and started to look for a small bay to spend the night. We had just about given up hope of spending a quiet night when we sighted a small boat passing through the reef ahead, about three miles away, and marking the spot in our heads we altered course towards it. The passage through the reef was not visible until we were nearly on it and the bay opened out before us. The foaming breakers rolled over the reef, the blue water stretched out embracing the palm-lined shore that carried on, winding back through low, chiselled hills to be lost from sight at the foot of tall, rugged mountains. The setting sun reflected back into the bay, beckoning an invitation that we would not have time to accept. There would be no shore leave here. Through the reef we raced toward the nearest point of land trying to beat the fast closing darkness. We used the leadline as we went, but the water remained too deep for anchoring right up to the shore. Backing out, we turned around and ran back towards the reef and anchored in shallow water just off the inner reef, five hundred yards from the entrance. While we were still swinging slowly around on our chain, Bill dived over the side and swam down, jammed the fluke of the anchor in a hole in the coral and we were safe enough in the calm water for the night. Duff already had the stew simmering on the stove and, after a good meal, it was great to be able to sit on deck, after all the noise and bustle of Tahiti, and enjoy the peace and quiet of the evening and watch the moon come up big and full from the sea.

That night I had my first good sleep for ten days and I knew nothing from the time my head touched the pillow until I heard the yell for breakfast. By eight o'clock we were already through the reef and pushing out from the island under motor. Reluctantly we turned it off to save petrol after an hour's running. The wind was still heading us and for six hours we rolled around in very big swells. We sailed when we could with the favourable winds that lasted only as long as the squalls that brought them. One thing in our favour was a strong current slowly taking us away from the island to seaward and it was not until four o'clock in the afternoon that we cleared land, picked up the true wind and at last got on our way. It was blowing fairly strong and we were taking the seas on the beam and were being thrown around quite a bit. Soon things were back to normal with stuff jumping out of their racks and brackets, and pepper and mustard all over the floor. When the first rays of sun lit the morning sky we were once again alone on the sea heading for Fiji, that is until the wind forced us to change our minds. Right on the nose it would not have been worth the effort and we decided to sail to Tonga instead. Bill went down below to plot our new course on the chart to Vava'u.

The trip to Tonga was the same as most of our passages, a little rough and a little smooth. We were getting closer to home with each passing day and that was the main thing. Water was again our problem. Our main water tank was emptying quickly and we spent many arduous hours

Sailing into sheltered waters, Tonga.

trying to locate a leak until the truth dawned on us: it was all the good food we had brought onboard, it took too much water to cook it.

Bill took his sextant on deck each midday for the noon sightings, and then it was my turn. Down below, we compared readings and Bill plotted our position across the chart day after day until we saw clouds that were not moving hanging over the sea. It seemed to take forever, but then we could make out a dark mass below them. We were anxious to reach the Friendly Islands before dark and as the wind picked up a little the 'Grey Dragon' slowly moved across a turquoise sea toward the emerald island. As if to greet us, a school of porpoises swam around our boat. The light was fading fast when Duff spotted the opening in the reef. He swung the lead, there was plenty of water, but where do we anchor? The twilight slipped into darkness. Our sails down, we motored towards the shore. The sound of the waves breaking on the coral filled us with great trepidation. In front of us I saw a light, and then another. They were torchlights. Soon there was a dozen and then a score and more, but what were they doing, warning us to keep clear or guiding us in? When Bill decided we were close enough, over went the anchor. We swung around and the back of the boat was much too close to the coral for my liking. The anchor was holding well and it was dangerous to move in the dark, so we decided to stay put.

We spent a terrible night with an anchor watch most of the time. In the morning Bill took the dinghy ashore and picked up a Tongan who spoke good English and had volunteered to guide us to a bay inside the island. There was very little wind and the sea was like glass. We could see the beautiful colours of the coral passing under our keel in about twenty to thirty feet of water. We also noticed a square, iron water-tank lying on a patch of white sand below these clear waters. While we were motoring past the steep cliffs, our Tongan friend explained about the lights. A month ago a yacht had left Tonga for New Zealand with seventeen Tongan boxers onboard who were going to fight there. No one had heard from them since, and the people on the cliffs thought and hoped that we were the boxers returning. Our pilot took us into a pretty, sheltered bay where we anchored and the Tongan was taken ashore with our thanks. We cleaned up our boat and put our wet things out to dry. While we were doing our chores a man in a canoe paddled up to the boat. His clothes were in tatters, with patches over patches. He wanted whatever he could get but we had very little to give him. He explained that the island had been devastated by a cyclone, and when we had a good look around we could see many of the palm trees had no tops and breadfruit trees had been blown over. A lot of the small trees had their leaves stripped and their fruit gone. The effect on a small island would make life difficult for years to come for all those who lived on it.

It was time for us to go ashore, the dinghy was in the water, taking up a little. The three of us got into it for a 'might get there' trip, one rowing, one bailing, one praying. When the bow touched the beach and we stepped out, dressed in our clean shorts, we did not get far. A big Tongan policeman, with his arms folded, informed us that we could not go ashore without a shirt on. He looked like a sumo wrestler, and we could only nod and get back in the dinghy for a 'hope we make it back' trip. Later, when walking around the island, suitably dressed, we had a look at the market. Not as good as Tahiti, but basic food was available and the shops were waiting to take our money. I did buy something, a tapa cloth, twelve by twelve with 'WELCOME TO THE QUEEN' on it. Bill and Duff said that I should not be left ashore alone! Most of the Tongans I saw were stocky and some a little heavy. No doubt their diet of starchy food, tapioca and sago (or frogs eyes as I called it) had something to do with it. When I asked a smiling Tongan where I could get a beer he informed me "no beer, no alcohol here, you can only drink kava".

After fighting the urge for a few days, Duff and I went ashore to learn the finer points of kava drinking. First you had to get the kava roots, and the priest was the only person who had some. I am amazed how these sin bos'ns get their fingers in all the best pies. Off I went to see him. He was a nice enough chap and worried about his flock. Money changed hands and I came away with the roots that did not impress me at all. The next step was a bit tricky, as we had to find a house with a young Tongan lass willing to crush the roots. Duff turned on the charm and, in no time, we were inside a house with a lass bending over a kava bowl that looked as if it had soapy water in it. She kept crushing and squeezing the juice through her fingers, while dad and mum kept a good eye on Duff and me through the doorway. The lass smiled and passed half a coconut full of kava to each of us. To say I have tasted worse is true, but not often, and when the bowl was empty I realised my tongue was numb. With the kava gone and the small talk finished, Duff and I thanked the lass and made our way out into the light and back safely to the boat.

A couple of days later Duff had the urge to try a little more kava, so ashore we went. Duff found a willing lass after a couple of knock-backs, and we were shown into a room. The kava bowl was very ornate and the lass skilled at making the juice, and in no time our coconut cups were full. The bowl emptied quickly, so we made our thanks and were on our way. Back on board Bill listened to our story and then informed us this was how you courted a girl here. There and then I decided that my kava-drinking days were over.

Duff, the keenest fisherman onboard, was not having too much luck and, when we went ashore and were told that some of the islanders had thought we were Russian spies, we considered that perhaps it was time to leave. The only thing that brightened up our day was watching the Tongan girls bathing in the sea, not far from our boat, in the late afternoon. Our binoculars had never had so much use. With what little money we had left we stocked up mainly with native food, and spent some time squaring the boat away.

We were under no illusions, the next leg of our trip was going to be a tough one. 'Variable winds' mean wind from any point of the compass, including no wind at all and other nasties. Captain Voss sailed his Red Indian canoe around the world, but had his worst weather off New

Zealand where he lost a man overboard. There were seventeen Tongans unaccounted for, and we were the first vessel going south since they disappeared. We discussed at great length what we would do. Our chart showed there was a reef between Tonga and New Zealand called Minerva. Surely they would have given the reef a wide berth, but it had to be suspect. We agreed that the course we sailed should take us close to Minerva, and planned our arrival for midday to see if we could find the reef. We kept a good lookout for any unusual flotsam, in case the vessel had broken up at sea. There could be a dinghy with survivors in it. We waited a day or two for favourable winds, then left the shelter of the harbour and turned our bow towards home. The green island slowly became smaller and smaller, and soon when I looked around it was gone. We were alone once more.

Chapter Eighteen

Homeward Bound

We saw nothing unusual as we sailed along our course. Duff told us he had seen a forty-four-gallon drum float past in the dark but the seas and wind were up and he did not call us. It would have taken a long time to tack back and we may not have seen it again. Closer to the reef, we reduced sail to allow Bill to take his sight and we reached the position of the reef early in the afternoon. We hove-to and the three of us searched as best we could, but in vain, as we saw only rolling seas stretching to the horizon on all sides. We became uneasy. Was it still ahead, was it to port or starboard? We decided to sail on and keep a very good lookout. We saw nothing, and when darkness fell I was glad we were past Minerva. With the clouds obscuring the stars it was one of those nights when the sky and the sea become one, and the boat sailed along into a black void.

As we approached the top of the North Island of New Zealand, the stormy weather became more frequent. We decided to sail down the west coast to Tasman Bay, and I was looking forward to seeing the extinct volcano Mount Egmont, over eight-thousand-feet high with its perpetually snow-covered top which can be seen for 100 miles at sea. However, this was not to be. The 'Grey Dragon', despite all our efforts, was blown from the west coast, off cape Maria van Diemen, over to the east coast. We fought our way south, day after day, and sleep was almost impossible. Duff still managed to cook a hot meal, holding the pressure-cooker on the stove with one hand and hanging on for dear life with the other. At one period, in the height of these September storms, we sailed

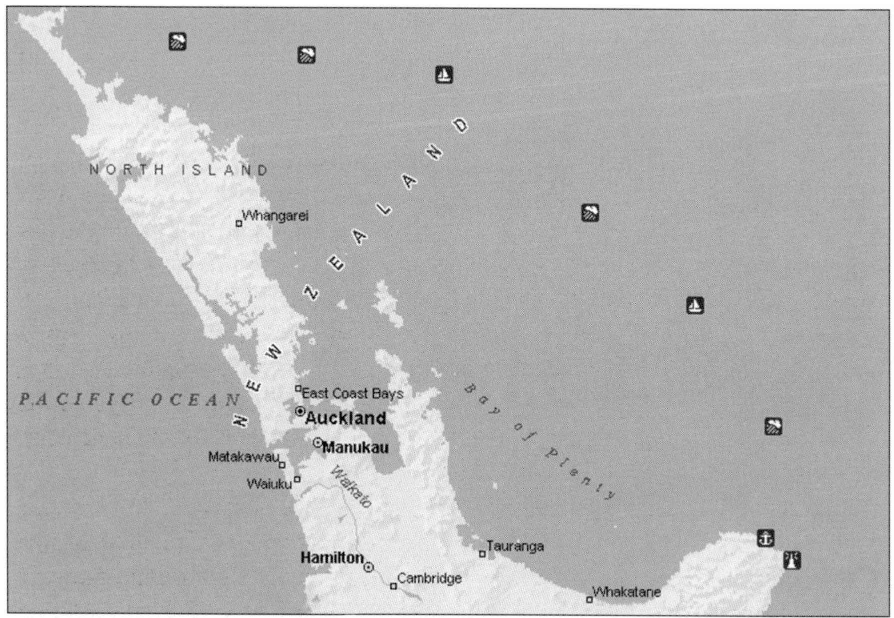

Hicks Bay, East Cape, New Zealand.

sixty miles in seven days. We saw the lights of what we thought was Auckland in the far distance, but were not tempted and sailed on.

On Saturday, September the 15th, our barometer dropped ominously and we were hit by gale-force winds in the Bay of Plenty area. Because the winds were taking us south we did not follow our usual practice of heaving-to. There was one spinnaker up and the boat was not too uncomfortable. Then, off the land came some sort of mini-tornado. All hell broke loose. In the twinkling of an eye, the sheet holding the spinnaker snapped. I called down to Bill 'she's gone', and when I looked up there was nothing left. Bill and Duff put up a staysail but it also would not hold, they then set a small storm-jib and we carried on with a big warp over the stern to break the seas. With this sail set we managed to clear East Cape with visibility almost nil and the usual strong tides to battle. The wind was so strong that the spray being whipped up made the sea appear to be smoking. Our boat would crest the huge waves and go down the other side like a surfboat, the momentum carrying it up the next one and down into the valley of water again, the tiller thrumming like a live thing under my palm. We all knew what would happen if she broached, but that which sets the course of the stars held us in the palm of His hand. I confess I was getting stubborn and refused to hand over the tiller to either Bill or Duff, but Neptune just smiled. He knew, and after eight hours I handed the tiller over.

When the wind veered to the north-west, the 'Grey Dragon' hove-to off East Cape. As soon as we were able we moved towards land and Bill sighted the light off the Cape at 10 p.m. The yawl hove-to again until Sunday morning. Down below in my bunk I listened to the roar of the waves. One moment I was horizontal, the next almost standing on my head. The sea followed the wind down, and by first light the weather had improved a lot. We had been at sea twenty-five days since leaving Tonga and needed to take on fresh water. We sailed in towards Te Araroa, but the closer we got we realised that the rollers would make it too difficult. In the morning, the wind swung around on the nose and we made the decision to pull into Hicks Bay.

It looked sheltered enough as we came abreast Matakaoa Point and, when we started to sail into the bay, the blue water became brown and by the time our sails were down it was almost mud. It was the run-off from the storms and the tornado that had just lashed the area, and was coming down the Wharekahika River. We could not see the bottom so we used the lead as we motored in toward a small jetty at the northern end of the bay. We tied the 'Grey Dragon' to land, and just looked at each other. What passed between us was unspoken. We had reached the 'Land of the Long White Cloud' and were close to home.

As we hung our gear up to dry, and cleaned up the boat, a car came towards us along the road to the jetty. A tall man got out and spoke to us in an American accent. I heard Duff say to Bill "I hope we haven't stuffed it up and landed in America". It was Arnold Look, a keen yachtsman, formerly of Rhode Island. He was a school-teacher and he and his wife were in New Zealand for two years. When he heard where we had come from he invited us to his home for a warm shower and a home-cooked meal. Both were very welcome and the offer was not refused. Our boat was safe at the jetty for a couple of hours, and once we were in the car it did not take long to reach their house overlooking the bay. His wife was charming, and their children had plenty of questions for us. The meal was beaut, but when it was finished we took our leave, headed back to the boat and motored out into the bay to anchor. Arnold asked if we would mind coming to the school early in the afternoon and telling the children about our trip.

The three of us rarely left the boat together, as we preferred to leave one onboard. However, we agreed to visit the school and were all picked up around two in the afternoon. I took the Tongan tapa along to show the children and soon we were looking into a sea of young faces as they threw questions at us: what did we eat, how did we sleep, what did we do all day. I told them about some of the islands we had visited. Duff told them about the Galapagos Islands and Charles Darwin, how he studied the animals and birds there, thus arriving at his theory of evolution by natural selection in the struggle for existence. Bill told them about navigation. While Duff and Bill were talking, I looked at the Maori children in the class. Some of them could have been direct descendants of Hoturoa, the chief who commanded the canoe Tainui, or Tama te Kapua, who commanded the canoe Arawa, on the migration voyage from Hawaiki in AD1350. They landed at Whangaparaoa just around the point from Hicks Bay after following Kupe's sailing instructions given centuries before – 'Sail to the right of the setting sun, sail towards the bright star'. This, of course, would depend on the time of the year, early November it would be to the left. They watched the waves, the clouds and birds to reach their destination. Most of these children would have some seafaring blood in their veins. They stood and thanked us warmly as we left, and soon we were in the car with Mrs McConnell, of Te Araroa, on our way back to the boat.

When the car reached the headland overlooking the bay we realised that the 'Grey Dragon' had moved and was not riding as she should be. As we were looking for a safer anchorage we saw her getting closer to the shore. Full of concern, we raced down and arrived as she went aground. The three of us climbed over the rocks and plunged into the water. Reaching the yawl we combined our strength, to push her off into deeper water, all to no avail. Bill went around the stern and I around the bow. We followed the anchor chain out and our hands met at the anchor. Feeling the upper fluke we realised that the chain had somehow wrapped around the top fluke. I looked at Bill and the despair on his face mirrored my own. We dragged the anchor out into deeper water as far as we were able, and Bill dived down and buried the fluke as deep as he could in the sand. Duff was already onboard down below, trying to pump the water out. We had always known the boat's weak point. The cockpit floor was not sealed completely, the centre of it had to be lifted to crank our motor over. The waves were breaking over the cockpit, filling it and draining into the boat. Bill tried to block it by covering it with a sail, but the waves found a way around it. Down below I bailed while Duff pumped, that is

Going ...

when he was not clearing a blockage which was expected under these conditions. The water sloshing around below was picking up everything that was loose. The roll of the boat, combined with the water, was forcing lockers open and spilling their contents.

The 'Grey Dragon' had gone ashore at four o'clock in the afternoon, and we fought for three hours to save her. After the tropics, we all found the water bitterly cold and it sapped our strength and impaired our mental ability. Then a ray of hope, a fishing-boat came into the bay. It was a Gisborne boat, the 'Olwyn', which was trawling in the area.

Going ...

Constable Milne, of Te Araroa, had contacted it and the fishing-boat reversed slowly towards us. The trawler came in as close as the skipper dared. The three men onboard tried to launch a small boat but it was too rough. I watched a man dive over the stern with a rope. He swam through the surf with it as Duff and Bill swam out to meet him. I made my way to the bow, while the boat tried to throw me in the water with its motion. Bill and Duff pulled the rope in and attached to it was a wire rope. Bill passed the eye up to me and I put it around the Samson post in the bow. The fishing-boat, belching black smoke as her motor roared, took up the slack. The bow turned slightly and I thought the yawl would pull free, but instead it pulled the Samson post out and left a hole two feet round in the deck. Our boat, more than half full of water, was immovable. The fishermen offered to try again but we said no. I guess we could have tried a pull from the top of the mast to try and heel her over, as we still hoped to salvage her and Bill was more than capable of repairing her. We thanked the brave fishermen who had risked their own boat to try and save ours and watched them disappear around the headland in the fading light. Once it was dark there was very little that we could do.

Before we left the boat that night, I climbed aboard and went below. The water was up over my waist, and I stood there in the darkness listening to her timbers creaking and groaning, and I caressed them with my hands while tears rolled down my cheeks. Suddenly, I heard a strange sound and went forward. My mouth opened in surprise – there was the fourth member of our crew, our canary – fluttering around his cage – terrified. How could we have forgotten him – he had lifted our spirits a hundred times with his songs. He had sailed thousands of miles and had his share of sleepless nights. I took him off the boat, away from all the noise, and nursed him on my lap on our trip back to the teacher's house. The children were pleased to see him, but it was way past his bed time and he was soon asleep on his perch. None of us slept well that night, not knowing what the morning would bring.

We were back down at the boat as soon as the light allowed us. Our yawl looked intact; she was holed, but that could be repaired. The tide was still coming in and the waves were crashing into her, sending spray half-way up her mast. We knew that we would have to wait until the tide receded, to take our things off and salvage her. Sitting on the rocks high above our boat, it was like being in a colosseum looking down at a lone gladiator fighting unbelievable odds. The 'Grey Dragon's' keel had been laid in the same year as mine, and as I watched I thought of the shipwright at Upham's boat-yard in Brigham, Devon. His selection of oak and pitchpine had been careful. This boat had been built when craftsmen had pride in their work. A boat may not have a soul as such, but it has an aura, as do we, that is slowly built up over the years by the thoughts and energy of all those who worked, lived and sailed in her These vibrations impregnate the boat, much the same as paint and varnish, and I always felt good, positive vibes around her.

After three hundred waves there is always one wave that is three times the size of those preceding it. I saw such a wave coming and I thought 'stuff you, Poseidon'. It was as if he had heard me and grasped the yawl's mast and drove it through the bottom of the boat. It was a mortal wound, but she did not surrender. The next big wave roared in and crashed on her already weakened bow, there was a tearing sound and the bow opened wide. I heard Bill and Duff gasp – the unthinkable had happened. As the wave receded, it sucked all our belongings out through the gaping hole, mattresses, clothes, personal belongings, etc. All our signal flags arranged themselves in a last message and floated over the waves out to sea. Another three-hundredth wave came roaring in

Gone ...

through the hole in the bow much the same as they do in a blow-hole. The compressed air and water had nowhere to go. The cabin top and sides lifted off neatly and cleanly, like the head of a man on a guillotine. The three of us sat and watched our boat being dismembered before our eyes, piece by piece, plank by plank. Our yawl had carried us safely twelve thousand miles, she had met storm after storm head on, her bowsprit spearing the waves like a needle, splitting them so that the white foam washed down her sides. As the timber broke and splintered, the smell of the pitchpine was released to caress our nostrils and drift off into the NZ bush.

The Good Book states that 'as you do to others so will be done unto you'. Perhaps we all were ship-wreckers in a past lifetime and now it was our turn to feel the pain and anguish. There was a hint of fate, or karma, here. Our boat was wrecked twelve months to the day since we left England. The end had been swift and we sat in silence. The bowsprit was broken, the 'Grey Dragon' was no more. We could have been wrecked a number of times during our long trip, and would have probably lost our lives, at least here in New Zealand we only lost our boat.

We followed the sea down over the rocks and onto the sand, where wreckage lay strewn over a wide area. Duff found our barrel barometer wedged under a rock and we gave it to the schoolteacher to repair and keep. Bill found a bottle of whiskey buried in the sand, five more out of the twelve were found and sold to the R.S.L Club to help warm the Anzac diggers on a cold winter's night. They will now raise and lower their flag on our mast, which has become their flagpole. The Maoris living close by salvaged everything they could use, wire, rope, timber, etc. and went off carrying the cabin top and sides. I hope it did not end up being a fowlhouse, as it deserved better. There was very little else left for us but before I left the beach, I found the small, wooden Maori tiki I had screwed on the bow at the start of the trip. It had come home.

The people around the area took up a collection for us, and the local store sent us some food and clothes, which was very kind of them. The local paper ran a story of the wreck, and this brought two results. A yacht owner came over from Auckland and bought our motor. The next day, when I answered a knock on the door at the teacher's house, there stood a Customs officer. "I have come for your canary" he said, and when I asked why, "it has not been in quarantine" he replied. "I will have to

Despair.

destroy it." I could not believe what I was hearing. I told him that the bird had been in quarantine for twelve months on the boat, but he was not interested. I tried to move past him outside, where I was going to let the bird go, but he would not let me pass. He asked for the bird again, and I put my left hand into the cage and held its tiny body. With my right hand I removed its head and held the bird out to him. He felt my anger, saw the fire in my eyes, and took a few steps backwards, turned and left. I put the tiny body in the wood stove and was left with the smell of burning feathers. There would be no canary for Julie, our Maori princess, back in Pokororo. It was to be our gift to her for all the kindness that she had shown us.

There and then I decided it was time to leave Hicks Bay. I left the Tongan tapa for the teacher. Bill and Duff thought they may stay another few days. The next morning I went down to say my good-bye to what was left of the boat. All that remained was the keel and some iron ballast. Bill and Duff agreed we would send a telegram to England to the people we had bought the 'Grey Dragon' from saying 'arrived safely,' which we had. We had kept the promise we gave them when we bought their boat.

With my pack on my back, I hitch-hiked down the Awatere Valley, then to Gisborne, and then down to Wellington, sleeping where I could when darkness overtook me. I caught the ferry over to Picton and it proved to be a rough crossing, almost losing a caravan that had broken loose over the side. When the ferry turned into Queen Charlotte Sound, the water was calm, the bays that we passed were beautiful and I could not help seeing the 'Grey Dragon' anchored in them. That night I slept at Tuamarina, not far from the spot where on the 17th June, 1843, the Pakehas tried to arrest the Ngati Toa chief, Te Rauparaha, over a land dispute. Unfortunately, one of the first few shots killed Te Rangihaeata's wife (Te Rauparaha's daugher) and utu was demanded. Twenty-two were killed for their folly, but no ghosts bothered my sleep that night. Once or twice I woke up and could feel the movement of the boat and hear the slap of the waves on the hull, but it was like a lullaby to a baby and back to sleep I went, thinking that with a bit of luck tomorrow I would be home. From Nelson I could see my beloved hills and snow-capped mountains across the sparkling, blue waters of the bay. From Motueka one of the farmers going home dropped me off at the swing bridge crossing the river.

I stopped to watch a trout, lying in ambush in the crystal-clear water. All around me there was new life, the poplar trees along the river were

Mount Arthur, Graham Valley, New Zealand.

wearing their new green leaves after the winter, and the scent of spring flowers filled the air. I knew that this is what I would have to do, copy nature and start anew. I remembered the sign on the small country church long ago –'Disappointments should be Cremated not Embalmed' – and I walked off the bridge and up the dusty road. I was wrong about the time I had spent at the mine, it had been worth it. I passed the tobacco-seed beds covered with white calico. On the other side of the road I watched a ewe bonding with her new-born lamb. The air blowing across the snow on Mount Arthur or Huka Papa, 'The Father of Snow', as the Maoris called it, had a crispness to it. I had completed the circle; Bill and Duff would do so in a short while. For me the 'blue water dreaming' was over. There would be other dreaming, as there always is, and I thought of the warning from the sages of old – be careful of what you wish for, what you dream, what you visualise, for it will be fulfilled. Bill and Duff arrived a few days later, and their circle was complete. There were old mates to see, parties to go to, beer to drink and stories to tell.

Glossary

ABEAM An object is said to be abeam when it is at right angle to the centre line of the yacht.

ANTIFOULING Paint applied to the underside of the boat which prevents weed and barnacles from growing.

BATCH Workers accommodation, usually two rooms.

BEAM Width of the boat.

BEATING TO WINDWARD A yacht cannot sail directly into the wind, so if her destination lies upwind this can only be reached by sailing "tacks" or zigzag.

BILGE The curved part of the boat's hull beneath the water where it turns towards the keel. Inside the boat it is covered with floorboards.

BLOCK A sea term for a pulley.

BOBSTAY A wire or chain from the outer end of the bowsprit to the bottom of the bow.

BOOM GAFF A wooden spar that holds the top of the mainsail. Gaff jaws fit around the mast. This boom can be raised or lowered when reefing but is subject to wear in light winds.

BOOM A wooden spar running horizontally from the mast to which the bottom of the mainsail is attached.

BOOMED-OUT A jib can be held out by rigging a boom on the opposite side to the mainsail so that it will catch more wind when running.

BOWSPRIT A spar projecting from the bow of a sailing vessel for holding the jib.

BUCKJUMPER An unbroken horse trying to throw its rider off.

BUMPKIN A beam or spar projecting outward from the hull of a vessel for extending a sail.

BURGEE Triangular-shaped identification flag flown by yachts.

CHAFE To rub, to wear out.

CLAP A sexually transmitted disease.

COPRA The hard flesh of a coconut.

CROSS TURNS OVER The stars of the Southern Cross turn a circle in the sky and is used by Australian drovers so they will be out of bed before dawn.

COPSE A thicket of small trees and bushes.

GRID SETTING A circle on top of the compass having two lines that can be altered to the course to be steered.

GUNNEL The upper edge of the side of a vessel. When sailing hard the gunnel can often be under water.

GUNWALE The same as gunnel. Where the guns rested.

HAKA A Maori war dance.

KILN A building in which an oil-fired system generates heat and steam to dry tobacco.

M.T.B. A war-time motor torpedo boat.

MIZZEN The shorter mast of a yawl aft of the cockpit and rudder.

MOB A large number.

NEPTUNE Roman God of the Sea.

POSEIDON Ancient Greek God of the sea.

PREVENTER STAY A rope stopping the mainsail and boom from swinging over in a gybe and possibly hurting someone or breaking gear.

SALTINGS The upper reaches of a river.

SEA COCK Valve fitted to any pipe where it passes throught the boat's hull.

SCUPPERS Drains around the edge of the deck.

SHEET Rope attached to the sails for adjusting their angle to the wind.

SHROUDS Wires which support the mast laterally.

SPINNAKERS Voluminous sails used when running downwind.

STANDING RIGGING Wire ropes including stays and shrouds used to support the mast.

STAYSAIL A second headsail set between the mainsail and the jib.

STORM-JIB A small sail made out of strong material for use in bad weather.

STREAM THE LOG An instrument towed behind the boat recording the distance travelled.

SWELL Long waves remaining well after the wind that created them has gone.

TARANAKI GATES Wire gates that are used in New Zealand.

UTU Maori word meaning recompense.

WARP A rope towed behind the stern of a yacht in a half circle to break up the following seas.

WEATHER SIDE The side on which the wind is blowing.

WOOLLOOMOOLOO A bay in Sydney Harbour where warships tied up.

YAWL A yacht that has a sail aft of the steering position.

Postscript

Some years later I read in a New Zealand newspaper that two skin-divers had found a square, iron tank, like the one the 'Grey Dragon' passed over, under the cliffs in Tonga. It turned out to be a strongroom, all that was left of a pirate ship which had been wrecked. It contained half-a-million pounds of treasure.

When the 'Grey Dragon' hove-to on the position of Minerva Reef, we had no idea that the 17 Tongans had been there for two months, living in the wreck of a Japanese fishing-boat, distilling fresh water out of salt and living off the reef. They were building a canoe from the timber inside the boat, and when it was finished two of the group, a father and son, sailed 1600 miles to Fiji only to be wrecked on the outer reef, leaving them to swim ashore. The father was swimming well ahead when his son got into difficulties. The agonising decision had to be made, turn back and save his son and risk them both being drowned, or continue on and save the rest of the men on the reef. He continued on and reached the beach. His son drowned, and most of the Tongan boxers were rescued after spending three months on the reef, a story of courage, sacrifice and seamanship.

The voice that warned me three times to switch the motor off as we were coming into the Galapagos Islands in heavy fog, is by no means unique. In 1989, a twenty-two-year-old Australian girl set off alone in an outrigger canoe to paddle around a small island in the Philippines. However, a strong current slowly carried her out to sea, despite all her efforts. It was getting late in the day and, as she did not wish to spend a night at sea, she was preparing to swim to the beach when a voice spoke to her for the first time. It warned her 'not to leave the canoe'.

That night she survived a frightening storm, and the next day the seas, generated by the wind, capsized the outrigger. As her gear was floating away the voice spoke to her for the second time telling her to 'get her flippers' which she did. Michelle endured another night clinging to the outrigger of her upturned canoe, and prepared for death. In the darkness and despair the voice spoke to her for the third time telling her 'she was not going to die'. Michelle survived the storm, immersion, sharks, sun and thirst for three days, and had drifted over 160 kilometres before she was seen by one of the crew of a fishing-boat that hove-to some distance away. It was a twenty minute swim to the boat, and without her flippers she would not have made it

Not far from where my wife and I now live a helicopter with two people on board crashed into the sea. The pilot was knocked unconscious. His companion undid the seat belt, brought him to the surface and they began to swim towards shore. The pilot began to slip beneath the waves and his companion dived down and brought him to the surface a number of times. Eventually, he saw that the pilot's eyes were glazed and beginning to lose their light – he was dying. Forced to release the dead pilot, he was now alone, and in despair he began to swim towards a tanker anchored some miles away. He heard the now-dead pilot's voice telling him not to swim towards the ship but to swim across the waves towards land, and the pilot continued to guide and encourage him until he felt the sandy beach under his feet.

I have investigated these uncharted waters and have experimented with and practised meditation. The outcome of it all is that I have learnt a philosophy worth more than all the gold found in the pirate ship's strongroom. The Good Book tells us 'seek and ye shall find', and I use the Buddhist principle of believing nothing until you have tested it for yourself – but then that is another story.

It is now forty-one years since the 'Grey Dragon' was wrecked and all three of us who came out from England in her are still alive and well, although scattered as we were before we first met. The three of us worked on different tobacco farms in the valley, and it was there that Bill Corbett and I met our wives.

Bill spent three years on Cos Newman's farm building a ferro-cement, 36-foot double-ender yacht which he called 'Beyond'. His blue water dream was to sail it back to England. However he met a 'Swiss Miss' called Rosa and they were married in 1972. Working as a boat-builder in Picton and Whangaeri Bill and his shipmate lived aboard their yacht for many years. Their twin daughters, Maria and Jeannette, shared their life until it was time to find a mooring ashore. They bought a couple of old army huts on a half-acre block in Keri Keri, Bay of Islands, and Bill used a lifetime of skills restoring them and creating 'Primrose Cottage'. He also made all his own furniture out of the Kauri timber salvaged from boats.

Bill Corbett is enjoying his twilight years with his wife Rosa, and together they tend their trees and garden. When the weather is warm they sometimes go sailing on a friend's boat, and Bill still repairs the odd dinghy free of charge to keep his hand in. I owe Bill a thank-you for urging me to finish these notes after so long. I am glad most of the notes and photos were sent back from the various ports we visited to Cos Newman in the valley. If not they, too, would have been lost in the wreck as were some of the latter ones together with my typewriter and camera.

Duff, after some years in New Zealand, travelled to Scotland, where he worked at the Glen Eagles Hotel as the head Cocktail Barman. These skills were again put to good use as he travelled further afield, working in both Amsterdam and Paris. Returning to Australia, he again went back to sea and worked in prawn trawlers for five years in the Gulf of Carpentaria, until the trawl on the boat 'John Silver' caught on a snag and rolled the trawler over. Duff spent two-and-a-half days in a dinghy with the owner and his wife, floating around the Gulf waiting to be rescued. He then worked in the outback before settling in Alice Springs for several years. It was here he met his wife Lynette. They have since moved to Brisbane, where he still works, and they live in their home at Scarborough.

I met my wife, Pam, in Pokororo, New Zealand. She had come to the tobacco fields as part of a working holiday, to have a change from her secretarial job in Adelaide, South Australia. It was an attraction of opposites. We were married in 1963, with most of my mates shaking their heads, saying it would not last, and forty years later we are still together. There have been lots of dreamings together, one of which was 'gold dreaming'. Shortly after we married we moved to Waikakaho Mine, out from Blenheim at the top of the South Island. John Hart discovered gold there in 1888, and 14 tons of the yellow metal was taken from across the range in Mahakipawa field. 36-ounce nuggets were followed down into the valley, but the water beat all who tried to reach bedrock, eighty feet below the stream. For two years we accepted the challenge. Pam cooked for twelve men on a coke stove and lived in conditions only her great-grandmother would have known. The fore-pole drives that I put in still stand today. The gold was found in small quantities in blue pug, but the glory hole eluded us.

Family duty called us back to Adelaide where I adapted to the stone jungle and worked at I.C.I. in the Power Services section for twenty years and was made a life member of the C.F.M.E.U. I joined a few sailing clubs and was at the Port Adelaide Club for over a decade – where I was Bar Manager for some time and Rear-Commodore for 12 months. I spent a number of years at the Royal South Australian Yacht Squadron, and a few years as a member of the North Haven club. There have been two boats, a 35-foot-wooden, motor sailer called 'Mary Anne' and the one I still own, a 32-foot fero RORC called 'Vintage Port'. She helps me keep in touch with nature, but I know I am only her caretaker as she will pass on soon to someone else. Pam and I have a daughter, Joanne, and a son, David, both of whom now live fulfilling lives of their own. Our son and his wife have their own consultancy business in Adelaide, and I am indebted to him and my wife for the help they have given me putting this story together. Our lives have been full and there are still more dream-ings to come – our four grandsons will see to that.

John and Pam Rodgers